CROON

The REVERB series looks at the connections between music, artists and performers, musical cultures and places. It explores how our cultural and historical understanding of times and places may help us to appreciate a wide variety of music, and vice versa.

reverb-series.co.uk

SERIES EDITOR: JOHN SCANLAN

Already published

The Beatles in Hamburg
IAN INGLIS

*Brazilian Jive: From Samba
to Bossa and Rap*
DAVID TREECE

*Crooner: Singing from the Heart
from Sinatra to Nas*
ALEX COLES

*Easy Riders, Rolling Stones:
On the Road in America, from
Delta Blues to '70s Rock*
JOHN SCANLAN

*Five Years Ahead of My Time:
Garage Rock from the 1950s
to the Present*
SETH BOVEY

Gypsy Music: The Balkans and Beyond
ALAN ASHTON-SMITH

Heroes: David Bowie and Berlin
TOBIAS RÜTHER

Jimi Hendrix: Soundscapes
MARIE-PAULE MACDONALD

The Kinks: Songs of the Semi-Detached
MARK DOYLE

The Monkees: Made in Hollywood
TOM KEMPER

Neil Young: American Traveller
MARTIN HALLIWELL

Nick Drake: Dreaming England
NATHAN WISEMAN-TROWSE

Peter Gabriel: Global Citizen
PAUL HEGARTY

*Remixology: Tracing the
Dub Diaspora*
PAUL SULLIVAN

*Song Noir: Tom Waits and
the Spirit of Los Angeles*
ALEX HARVEY

*Sting: From Northern Skies
to Fields of Gold*
PAUL CARR

*Tango: Sex and Rhythm
of the City*
MIKE GONZALEZ AND
MARIANELLA YANES

*Van Halen: Exuberant California,
Zen Rock'n'roll*
JOHN SCANLAN

CROONER

SINGING
FROM THE HEART
FROM SINATRA
TO NAS

ALEX COLES

REAKTION BOOKS

For Frank

Published by Reaktion Books Ltd
Unit 32, Waterside
44–48 Wharf Road
London N1 7UX, UK
www.reaktionbooks.co.uk

First published 2023
Copyright © Alex Coles 2023

Printed and bound in Great Britain by
TJ Books Ltd, Padstow, Cornwall

A catalogue record for this book is available from the British Library
ISBN 978 1 78914 766 7

Contents

Hollywood, California, 12 September 1943: dean of the crooners Bing Crosby puts a friendly arm around the shoulder of Frank 'The Swooner' Sinatra, as they meet for the first time. Although Sinatra sends the sub-deb set into comas, Bing still holds his own at the box office.

Introduction

Crooners are baritone singers who bare their emotion through popular song. While the classic tuxedo-clad figure of the mid-twentieth century typified by Frank Sinatra eventually reached a dead end on the easy listening cruise-ship circuit, the crooner has continued to evolve, operating at the progressive edge of popular music. Offering a veritable buffet of vocal delights, crooners have fashioned multiple voices with different emotive functions to elicit meaning, changing with – and indeed changing – the times. They have played a central role in constructing, taking apart and then reconstructing masculinity, becoming emblematic of a figure that we speak through in a way that is constantly redefined in dialogue with the shifting ages. Excelling at unguarded intimacy, the crooner has served as nothing less than our emotional ventriloquist for over half a century.

Instead of being historically defined, with fixed characteristics, the archetype of the crooner is plural and unfolds over time. From Scott Walker in pop and Barry White in disco to Grace Jones in reggae and Nas in hip hop, the development of the crooner has been neglected, having taken place under the guise of seemingly antithetical musical genres. Since every genre of music has its crooner, to overlook the major role the archetype has played would be to ignore what lies at the very centre of some of the most vital innovations in vocal music. No matter how dramatically they are reworked, there are a set of recognizable motifs and tendencies common to all crooners, irrespective of generation or geographical location. These turn on four distinct categories: the voice, the torch ballad (a ballad of unrequited love), the concept album (an LP with a consistent mood or theme) and the manipulation of the studio. Ensnaring the liquid vibrato of certain crooners in words is no small feat, but these categories help.

Neither a musicological study attempting to account technically for each crooner's voice nor a sociological analysis of the broader cultural triggers for the archetype, *Crooner* seeks to simultaneously describe the impact each voice has on the archaeology of the archetype.

In *Real Men Don't Sing* (2015), Allison McCracken traces the etymology of the word 'crooning', starting with the German word *croyn*, meaning to sing or speak in a low murmuring tone.[1] Later definitions describe the act of crooning as a lament, imbuing it with the potential for pathos.[2] Complicating this etymological definition, crooners each plot their own point on the graded arc running from pathos to bathos, the latter being understood as the humorous or trivial. Typified by the sheer transformative force of Sinatra's voice, between the 1940s and the late 1960s there is a greater strive towards pathos, with slips into bathos usually being unintended. From the early 1970s onwards, pathos has been increasingly treated as an aspect of style to be accessed precisely through bathos. Activating the trope of the crooner in both his song choice and dress, the camp sob in Bryan Ferry's voice in his cover of 'Smoke Gets in Your Eyes' (1974) underscores the song's lyrical conceit. As if in response to Sinatra's carefully constructed machismo, camp has become crucial to almost all successive crooners.

Parallel with the shift from pathos to bathos is the one from the sensual to the sentimental. Some crooners can even turn a sensual song into a sentimental one and vice versa, interpreting the same song in two entirely different ways. While Bobby Womack's 'Fly Me to the Moon' (1969) smoulders with eroticism, Tony Bennett's version from four years earlier is full of tenderness. Time can play a role in this transition, both in terms of the era the song originates from and was first performed in and the age and character of the voice interpreting it. Sometimes a crooner can even perform the same song two very different ways in two distinct eras. Dick Haymes singing 'It Might as Well Be Spring' with all the wistful joy present in his youthful voice in 1945 yields very different results to the darker version of the song cut just over a decade later when Haymes was in decline.

The artifice of the crooner is nowhere more pronounced than with the song of pathos itself: the torch ballad, an emotive song soaked with lament for unrequited love. The torch-ballad genre was initially associated with the female torch singers typified by Libby Holman, who just preceded male crooners like Rudy Vallée in the early 1930s. Gradually, the torch ballad was developed as a strand of the so-called American Songbook, with later numbers such as 'One for My Baby (and One More for the Road)', composed by Harold Arlen and Johnny Mercer in 1949, being perpetually reinterpreted by artists ranging from Billie Holiday onwards. As with the archetype of the crooner, instead of assuming the torch ballad to be limited by its historical definition, this book takes it to be a genre gradually defined over time. Proving to be one of the most fertile vocal vehicles of all, the torch ballad is fundamental to each of the crooners discussed in the following pages.

While Bing Crosby is perceived to be one of the founding figures of crooning, his torch ballads arguably lack the requisite emotional depth fundamental to the account of the crooner developed here. A duet performance of 'September Song' with Sinatra on a TV show in 1957 reveals why. Crosby's reading of the opening line from the first verse is wistful but sweet. Despite his early exchanges with Louis Armstrong, Crosby's voice remains unemotional and his treatment of the narrative relatively unfettered. It's as if Crosby is incapable of channelling weightier emotions. But when Sinatra enters with the

Libby Holman as photographed by Maurice Seymour, sometime between 1930 and 1950.

line about turning leaves to flame, everything changes; the history of crooning that this book charts begins. Though written by the same hand as the verse Crosby just sang, listeners can't help but find themselves caught up in the emotive narrative Sinatra spins with just these first few words. Partly, this is due to Sinatra's felicitous manipulation of the mechanics of singing: the listener is made aware of the air being drawn up from his chest, through his larynx, and then used to drive the way he emphasizes the word 'flame'. The sense of emotion Sinatra infuses the word with is extended in the next line with his emphasis of the word 'time'. Eschewing the languorous seduction that envelops his justly celebrated signature romantic ballads, Sinatra's superlative ability to act out the emotional drama in a torch ballad's lyric renders him their most innovative interpreter of the era. These emotions are enriched for being drawn from a diverse cultural pool. Operating as a subtle ethnomusicologist, Sinatra weaves together a tapestry of vocal techniques to access emotional cues from the perspective of other cultural backgrounds, particularly Italian Americans and African Americans, operating as a conduit to them for the listener.

In contrast to Crosby, who yielded only imitators (typified by Haymes and Perry Como), Sinatra has proved to be an important figure for successive generations of crooners. Even the most unlikely crooners, hip-hop musicians, engage directly with Sinatra – as explored in Bonz Malone's 1995 article for *Vibe* magazine, 'O. G.: Frank Sinatra Didn't Take Orders; He Took Over' – and Sinatra has been sampled and namedropped by everyone from Nas to Quentin Miller.[3] *Crooner* therefore also charts Sinatra's ongoing impact on successive generations of musicians, lending their engagement with him an intergenerational resonance that stretches out across gender, class and racial boundaries. Allowing the optic of the present to bring somewhat blurred moments of the past into crisp focus, each chapter identifies an aspect of Sinatra's oeuvre appropriate to the crooner being explored. Where Nick Cave's *The Boatman's Call* (1997) draws on the darkness of Sinatra's final LP of torch ballads *She Shot Me Down* (1981), Nas's *Life Is Good* (2012) lends the shift between speaking and singing on *Sinatra at the Sands* (1966) renewed relevance.

From this dialogue across genres and generations emerges a fresh argument that goes against the grain of received popular music historiography, which assumes Sinatra and the crooner's currency was depleted for good by the appearance of first, Elvis, second, the Beatles, and third, Bob Dylan.[4] First-hand accounts reveal this reading to be only partially accurate at best. To begin with, Elvis opted to return from the army in 1960 via Sinatra's TV show, and then followed the singer to Las Vegas at the turn of the next decade with endless versions of 'My Way'. Paul McCartney, too, communicated directly with Sinatra, replying to his request to make a demo of a song he'd previously written with his style in mind, as per 'When I'm Sixty Four'. 'It was a great moment when one of the engineers [at Abbey Road] said, "Paul, Sinatra's on the phone,"' recalls McCartney. 'And I was able to go, "Oh, I'll be there in a minute," touch a fader and then go off. And everyone would go, "Ooooo! Sinatra's on the phone!"' 'He was asking for a song,' continues McCartney, 'so I found the song ['Suicide'], made a demo and sent it to him.'[5] Ultimately Sinatra rejected the song, but just McCartney's impetus speaks volumes. Even before revisiting Sinatra's torch songs with his stream of recent LPs devoted to them, Bob Dylan was deeply engaged with Sinatra's music. 'I used to play the phenomenal "Ebb Tide" by Frank Sinatra a lot and it never failed to fill me with awe,' writes Dylan, '[because] when Frank sang that song, I could hear everything in his voice – death, God and the universe, everything.'[6] In the 1960s no one would have guessed that a folk singer could have these feelings about a crooner of the 1950s.

In *Performing Rites* (1996), Simon Frith explains how the voice can be described in musical terms, like any other instrument, as having a certain tone and timbral quality.[7] Produced physically by the movement of muscles in the chest and throat, to listen to a voice, argues Frith, is to listen to the sound of a body. While this is the case for all instruments, the voice draws attention to the activity of the body itself, seeming to give the listener access to it without mediation. The body of the crooner, optimized because of its physical absence, is assigned by the listener to a person with a distinctive gender, class and race depending on the precise timbre of their voice.[8] By using a certain tone of voice, crooners often adopt the persona of a vocal character in the guise of the protagonist of a song.[9] All of the crooners detailed in this book fashion their distinctive voices through a strategic blending of these four vocal categories identified by Frith (the voice, the torch ballad, the concept album and the manipulation of the studio).

In addition to the crooner's ability to compel us to identify with the character portrayed in a song, the sheer joy and vocal gymnastics the crooner entertains inspire the listener to try out these same sounds at home. This tends to strike closer to the bone than, say, the guitar, since we too have vocal chords capable of performing an approximation of the sounds made by the crooner. The pleasure derived from listening to crooners lies in the play made between being addressed by their voices and using their voices in turn to address someone else, real or imagined. In this sense, we take on the crooner's voice as our own – not just as an instrument but emotionally, by inhabiting the persona of the character being performed in the song.

The moment of the listener's transformation into a performer is affectionately captured by a scene in Sofia Coppola's *Lost in Translation* (2003): in a karaoke bar in Tokyo, Bill Murray's character,

Crooning to a crowd in *Lost in Translation* (dir. Sofia Coppola, 2003).

Bob Harris, sings Roxy Music's 'More Than This' (1982) longingly to Charlotte, the character played by Scarlett Johansson. As Bob reaches the chorus, so much feeling is put into the interpretation that the emotive force of each nuance of the lyric is fully registered, even though the singing is way off pitch. Interpreting the experience of this transformation, ethnomusicologist Charles Keil writes about his experience of this exact scenario, witnessing the scene in a karaoke bar in Tokyo. 'Watching people really getting worked up singing with the microphone,' Keil recounts, 'they get pumped up trying to sound like Frank Sinatra ... [and] enter in a participatory way the persona of the person they're trying to imitate.'[10] Whether through Sinatra, Ferry or any other crooner, the desire to transform from being a listener to a performer speaks volumes about the important social role that crooning continues to play. For both the performer and the listener, the early development of the archetype of the crooner is nothing less than an effective delivery system for emotion.

The way in which the archetype of the crooner can be worn as a mask surely accounts for the diversity of both performers and listeners who have chosen to identify with it, from presidents and punk rockers to mafia dons and miscellaneous pop stars. As a moderate liberal, John F. Kennedy's choice of Sinatra to not only provide his campaign song in the 1960 election – a rewrite of the previous year's 'High Hopes', no less – but curate the entertainment for his inaugural ball as president-elect for the Democrats plays through this logic. That exactly twenty years later Sinatra should be invited to repeat the gesture and organize Ronald Reagan's inauguration – singing 'Nancy' to the First Lady – means quite a different thing. By then Sinatra and the crooner archetype had swung to the right, to the Republican party. Both performer and listener were wearing the same mask as earlier, but what it meant to wear it had radically changed. Meanwhile, during the same twenty-year period, innovators such as David Bowie and Grace Jones worked to either 'androgenize' or warp the crooner's mask considerably. These two

Frank Sinatra sings and speaks at a rally for President Franklin Delano Roosevelt
sponsored by an independent voters' commission, 4 November 1944.

masks of the crooner – one frozen in time, the other in a process of
constant transformation – continue to be worn today but only the
former is considered in this book.

One of the key developments in the crooner of the past five
decades is an increasing, and even at times overbearing, tendency
to establish vocal individuality. Beginning with Sinatra (Chapter
One), this book follows with Scott Walker (Chapter Two); acceler-
ates with Barry White (Chapter Three), David Bowie (Chapter Four),
Bryan Ferry (Chapter Five) and Tom Waits (Chapter Six); and inten-
sifies with Grace Jones (Chapter Seven), Ian McCulloch (Chapter
Eight), Nick Cave (Chapter Nine) and Nas (Chapter Ten). Striving

to enhance the uniqueness of their vocal sounds can take up a large amount of a crooner's time. While stasis and inevitably parody can be the outcome, this tendency can also lead to a development like Bowie's in the 1970s, in which new facets of the voice are constantly revealed. More than any other singer, the Bowie of 1976 provides a hinge in time between the deeper history of the crooner's voice – reaching back to the 1930s and '40s – and forward to what follows in the late 1970s with the new wave voices of McCulloch and Cave.

The emphasis on the tone and timbre of the voice is partly explained by the general tendency for musicians to spend an increased amount of time in the studio from 1966 onwards. Where in the 1950s Sinatra would typically cut an entire album in three two-hour evening sessions, by 1966 innovative popular musicians began to spend an extended amount of time in the studio. Sound became sculpted rather than captured per se: besides being subject to various filters and manipulations of speed, a recorded vocal performance could be a composite of numerous takes, some with a gap of months in between. While the sound of the crooner has always been indivisible from the technology used to store and replicate it – true as far back as Crosby with his financing of the post-war shift to magnetic tape – the tools leave an increasingly opaque residue as the decades unfold. As this opacity increases, so does the listener's awareness of it.[11]

The use of autotuners in post-production is a contemporary example of this. Initially deployed in a subtle way by producers and engineers to alter vocals and correct occasional off notes, in the past decade and a half the autotuner has become a full-blown identifying characteristic, frequently resulting in a static and metallic vocal performance, particularly in ballad singing, when applied uniformly. Used to give certain vocal passages a contrasting texture, however, as in Kanye West's *808s & Heartbreak* (2008), the autotuner can produce engaging results. Since a discerning use of technology continues to be imperative to the development of the crooner's voice, the studio and its technologies are a sub-theme running right through this book, with each chapter offering a portal onto a crooner at work in a studio on a specific torch ballad. The action shifts from studios in Los Angeles, London and Montreux, all the way to Nassau, on to Liverpool and back again to LA. Each place is a home to the peripatetic shapeshifter that is the crooner.

Of all the technological equipment at their disposal in the studio, the defining instrument for crooners is undoubtedly the microphone. Following its introduction in the mid-1920s, it was the development of highly sensitive microphones in the 1950s that changed both the way crooners sang and the way they were recorded. Communicating sounds that normally imply intimacy – the hushed voice, the whisper – the microphone serves as an electronic extension of the crooner's voice box, a prosthetic device connecting the singer's voice to the listener's ear. Although it was as if Crosby seemed to be overheard by the microphone, Sinatra was the first crooner to play it, becoming dexterous in adjusting the proximity of his mouth to it.

Besides its use in the studio, manipulation of the mic is also a key part of the crooner's live performance. 'Young Sinatra famously clung to the mic stand,' writes Tracy Thorn in *Naked at the Albert Hall* (2016), 'twining his skinny body around it as if for support, or as if he were clutching at a lover.'[12] While up until the mid-1970s crooners treated the mic in much the same way as Sinatra in concerts, Bowie changed the way the mic was manipulated in performance. Where earlier crooners used the mic only as an instrument, with Bowie it became a crucial prop – literally so during his 1974 tour, when the mic was embedded in the telephone during the part of 'Space Oddity' when ground control is talking to Major Tom. By contrast, in early concerts, Cave almost seemed to abuse the instrument, while Nas uses it riotously as a megaphone to speak through. No matter how it is done, the mic is key to the crooner.

A degree of technical virtuosity and conceptual acuity is necessary to all crooners developing the nuances of their voices. Manipulation of the facial mask to shape sounds and display emotion is a strategic part of the crooner's expressive armature. Sinatra was singularly aware of both, establishing the fundamental working methods underpinning the output of the crooner. Key among them was phrasing. From trombonist Tommy Dorsey, whose band Sinatra joined prior to going solo in 1942, the singer learned how to sustain a legato ('bound together') phrase. More than anything else, this was the key to smooth and melodious singing, often sustaining eight bars without taking a visible or audible breath. Every time gravity attempts to bring a sung phrase down to earth, Sinatra projects it back up again, producing vertigo in the listener.

Just as crucial to the development of the crooner from the 1950s until today is Sinatra's prescient initiative to work in long form by pioneering what later came to be called the 'concept album'. While *The Voice of Frank Sinatra* (1946) was the first disc to contain a complete musical programme of songs recorded expressly for the LP, the Capitol LPs of the 1950s took this approach to new heights. However widely acknowledged it is that Sinatra picked a mood or an overall theme for ballad LPs from *In the Wee Small Hours* (1955) onwards, there has been less recognition of how each of his collections of torch songs is crafted with precision by plotting the progression of a narrative using carefully sequenced songs. From Sinatra's *Only the Lonely* (1958) to Walker's *Scott 3* (1969), Jones's *Living My Life* (1982), Cave's *The Boatman's Call* (1997) and up to Nas's *Life Is Good* (2012) more than fifty years after Sinatra, the crooner's handling of the concept album tends to be much looser: a definite theme is developed, but its contours and the narrative arc of the characters populating it remain sketchy. The result is a more open suite of songs, which prioritizes the flow of the voice.

Prior to the 1960s, crooners exclusively interpreted popular songs. Two singers could interpret the same song at the same time but with different results. The contrast between Dick Haymes's reading of 'The Way You Look Tonight' (1956) and Andy Williams's version (1966) highlights the fundamental differences between the two: where Haymes's version proceeds at a funereal pace and is shot through with a sense of regret, Williams's is upbeat and rife with a sickly sweet inertia. In the former, the object of the singer's affection is gone, while in the latter the object is very much present. This goes to the root of the fact that lyrics and melody are but a basis for interpretation by the performer. The key dynamic here is the one established between the melody and lyrics of a song and their interpretation by the individual crooner.

By the early 1960s the self-penned songs of figures emerging from French chanson, American folk, Brazilian bossa nova and the legacy of German Singspiel began to infiltrate popular music. From the mid-1960s, innovative performers started to almost exclusively sing their own material. Drawing on the text-heavy songs of Jacques Brel, Scott Walker is the first crooner to write his own songs in the English language. By the early 1970s this tendency had developed to such a degree that Bowie went one step further by inventing characters, including the Thin White Duke, to perform these self-penned songs. Cave extends this tendency from the 1980s onwards, progressing through a series of periods – including his LP of exquisite torch ballads, *The Boatman's Call* (1997) – and using his lyrical dexterity to explore various types of subject-matter from multiple narrative perspectives, recently giving way to a more atomized type of lyrical approach on *Ghosteen* (2019). Hip-hop's crooners such as Nas respond to the relationship between a written lyric and the voice by penning torch ballads like 'Bye Baby' (2012), in which the contours of characters seemingly premised on themselves is fleshed out.

Extending this exploration of a given character, film exerts a significant impact on our perception of the crooner. While in some cases film provides an important arena in which crooners have broadened their creative remit, it also contributes to our understanding of the role and character of crooners by providing theatricalized versions of them. This starts with the film *Crooner* (1932), a satire on the cultural perception of the crooner at the time. Sinatra frequently explored topics of a political bent largely absent from his singing, with films such as *The Man with the Golden Arm* (1955) and *The Manchurian Candidate* (1962), focusing on heroin addiction and political conspiracy, respectively, finding no equivalent in the subjects explored on his albums. A further indication of Bowie's role as a hinge in the development of the crooner comes with the way, in contrast to Sinatra, Bowie used film to explore issues parallel with those in his music, including *The Man Who Fell to Earth* (1976) and its enquiry into the psychological profile of an extra-terrestrial, and *Just a Gigolo* (1979), with its fascination with Weimar Berlin. From Bowie onwards, this became something of the norm; Waits's roles in *Rumble Fish* (1983) and *Down By Law* (1986) and Cave's in *Ghosts of the Civil Dead* (1989) and *Johnny Suede* (1991) correspond with those adopted in their songs. Film has also contributed to the fictive image of the crooner – made more complex by the fact that real crooners have played them on the screen, especially Sinatra in *Pal Joey* (1957). More recently, Mos Def plays a rapper in *Brown Sugar* (2001) and Kid Cudi a musical prodigy in *Scorpion* (2014). In *Blue Velvet* (1986) and *Buffalo 66* (1998), directors David Lynch and Vincent Gallo use the motif of the crooner as a ploy to inject either a more sexual or psychological dimension into their films. The character played by Dennis Hopper in *Blue Velvet* has a psychotic release whenever the song of the same name is sung to him by a crooner, and in *Buffalo 66* Ben Gazzara's character uses crooning in place of dialogue to communicate feelings he is otherwise unable to articulate.

While later generations of crooners may dress and sound different to Sinatra – lipstick, cross dressing, spikey hair or Nike trainers would have been as anathema to him as using an autotuner – the core purpose of assembling torch ballads together on an LP as a vehicle for the voice to express emotions remains constant.

1

Frank Sinatra : 'What's New?' (1958)

'Master 19257, Take One.' Bill Miller begins the piano intro, and
after a few seconds the take is halted and there is faint studio
chatter. 'Master 19257, Take Two.' The piano introduction is
completed, and a simple swell of strings spiral down, giving way
to a harp glissando and Sinatra's entrance at the verse.[1]

On the third take of 'Lush Life' attempted at Capitol Records's
studios on Sunset and Vine in Los Angeles in May 1958,
Sinatra made it all the way through to the chorus before it
all broke down. Finally, the song was rejected. Sinatra's failure to cut
'Lush Life' was a by-product of the ambition driving the LP *Only the
Lonely* (1958), which established a series of fundamental working
methods for the crooner.

Sinatra initiating a collaboration between lyricist Sammy Cahn
and composer Jimmy Van Heusen for the title track of *Only the Lonely*
is the nearest a crooner got to composing his own material in the
1950s. Of all the songwriters whose material Sinatra performed,
Cahn and Van Heusen understood the subtleties of his vocal timbre
the best. 'Sinatra's voice went through range changes,' explained
Cahn, '[going] from the violin with Axel [Stordahl]' in the 1940s
'to the sound underneath, the viola, with Nelson [Riddle]' in the
1950s.[2]

Cahn and Van Heusen's title song, *Only the Lonely*, sets a new
standard for the concept LP. Together the twelve songs making up
the LP clock in at almost the hour mark – around twenty minutes
longer than the average LP of the period – and provide Sinatra with
his most expansive canvas yet. Conceiving of it as a series of vignettes

exploring the different facets of loneliness, the LP develops a density of design unusual for popular music of the decade. Each song is carefully chosen and precisely sequenced, with the title song on Side 1 positioned first to set the scene for the narrative to come, and the closer on Side 2, Harold Arlen and Johnny Mercer's 'One for My Baby (and One More for the Road)', placed last to conclude it. Songs such as 'Angel Eyes', 'Guess I'll Hang My Tears Out to Dry' and 'Gone with the Wind' sit in between. Referring to both *Only the Lonely* and the torch ballad collection *No One Cares* (1959) that followed it, Sinatra describes his approach to the concept LP in detail:

> I get a short list of maybe sixty possible songs, and out of these I pick twelve and record them. Next comes the pacing of the album, which is vitally important; I put the titles of the songs on twelve bits of paper and juggle them around like a jigsaw until the album is telling a complete story lyric-wise. For example, the album is in the mood of 'No One Cares' – track one. Why does no one care? Because 'There's A Cottage For Sale' – track two . . . So on right through to the last track, which might be 'One For My Baby (And One More For The Road)' – the end of the episode.[3]

Producing one of Sinatra's most intimate vocal performances, including a subtle glissando each time the word 'baby' is sung, of all the tracks on *Only the Lonely* 'One for My Baby (and One More for the Road)' is the most complete in itself, operating like a stand-alone short story based around an intense conversation. Beginning with a stark piano played by Sinatra's frequent accompanist Bill Miller, the song's forlorn and slightly intoxicated protagonist addresses his interlocutor, Joe the bartender, by recounting a romance gone wrong. Sinatra explains the unique studio conditions in which the track was recorded:

something happened then which I've never seen before or since at a record session. I'd always sung that song before in clubs with just my pianist Bill Miller backing me, a single spotlight on my face and cigarette, and the rest of the room in complete darkness . . . [Dave Cavanaugh] knew how I sang it in clubs, and he switched out all the lights bar the spot on me . . . Dave said, 'roll 'em,' there was one take, and that was that.[4]

Crucially, in contrast to a live performance of 'One for My Baby (One More for the Road)' in a club wearing a tuxedo, its performance in the recording studio was not an end in itself but a means of transforming a transitory moment into an enduring track. As producer, Cavanaugh knew how to coax an optimum vocal performance from Sinatra that could stand up to repeated plays over the oncoming decades.

A composite of devices absorbed from several different sources, the essential principles of Sinatra's vocal technique on *Only the Lonely* produced myriad shadings, and formed the basis of the artifice underpinning the crooner's craft. Briefly outlined in the introductory chapter, one key source for this was trombonist Tommy Dorsey's ability to sustain a note, exploring a song by tying phrases together in a smooth progression, the continuity lending a new dimension to the melodic line. Since joining Dorsey in 1939, night after night, Sinatra observed the band leader's example and deftly translated Dorsey's skill on the trombone into vocal terms. 'I used to watch Tommy's back, his jacket, to see when he would breathe . . . I'd swear the son of a bitch was not breathing.'[5] Eventually Sinatra identified a small pin hole Dorsey kept open at the corner of his mouth, hidden by the trombone's mouthpiece, which allowed the band leader to breath discretely. Pulling back the cover shrouding Dorsey's technique, Sinatra developed a way to take a breath through the corner of his mouth, enhanced by the increased lung capacity built-up by swimming lengths underwater. The result was

Enrico Caruso, 1910.

a seemingly effortless ability to sustain a note. When guided by an acute emotional intelligence, this technical ability leads to an incredible range of expression. Treated as just an end in itself, this physical ability leads to technically impressive but vapid singing. Witness how Sinatra's contemporary Vic Damone delivers crooning-by-numbers on ballad LPs from the late 1950s and early 1960s such as *Linger Awhile with Vic Damone* (1962), recorded for Capitol.

Fullness is a crucial component of Sinatra's vocal arsenal, principally absorbed from recordings of the popular Neapolitan operatic tenor Enrico Caruso. Applied too liberally, fullness readily opens out onto machismo – witness the bravado of the self-aggrandizing 'My Way' (1969) – but used carefully, it increases the emotional range and impact of a song. On the recordings Caruso made for the Victor Talking Machine Company in New York between 1904 and 1920, the tenor's voice is deep and powerful – the first artist to lend the sound of the recorded voice a thick, three-dimensional quality. The same year that tenor Mario Lanza's portrayal of him in the film *The Great Caruso* (1951) was released, Sinatra channelled Caruso's fullness in an initial attempt at the torch ballad 'I'm a Fool to Want You' (1951) with arranger Axel Stordahl, the voice already having deepened from the sweet one usually associated with the Columbia years

(1943–52), but still far from realizing its full potential as it did in the Capitol years (1953–61). Sinatra's second attempt at the song five years later on the Gordon Jenkins-arranged *Where Are You?* (1957) is far more effective, enhanced by Capitol using the Neumann U47, a mic that seems to pick up every reverberation of the diaphragm. The fullness of Sinatra's now viola-like voice, with its attendant patina, was effectively harnessed by the singer, arranger and engineer: with the sonic register of the voice being lower, the emotional range it explored is also a number of shades darker. This time when Sinatra sang, it was deeply effective.

Sinatra pressed note-sustaining and fullness into the service of precise enunciation. A crucial part of his vocal technique, in sharp contrast to his speech (which firmly places him in Hoboken, New Jersey), precise enunciation was used by Sinatra to attain a state of apparent classlessness. Premised on the way Mabel Mercer, whom Sinatra heard on LP and in concert, gave equal weight to the lyric and melody of a song from the 1920s onwards, precise enunciation ensured the words contained in each phrase were immediately understood, with every comma and consonant being fully registered. But while they are faultless, Mercer's readings of popular songs lack emotional drama: each song maintains the same emotional pitch no matter its subject. Mercer read the lyrics more than she interpreted them.

By using enunciation precisely to serve the ends of interpretation, from the mid-1930s, Billie Holiday – born in 1915, the same year as Sinatra – developed a fresh approach to singing. 'I don't think I'm singing,' explains Holiday, 'I feel like I'm playing a horn. I try to improvise like Les Young, like Louis Armstrong or someone else I admire. What comes out is what I feel. I hate straight singing. I have to change a tune to my own way of doing it.'[6] Using her voice as a horn enabled Holiday to emphasize aspects of a melody by slurring and bending notes to realize the full dramatic potential of a song. 'Bending those notes – that's all I helped Frankie with,' commented Holiday, referring to the hours Sinatra spent watching her perform and the conversations they would have during their shows' intermissions.[7]

Using a vocal technique to access emotions from the perspective of other cultural backgrounds was crucial to Sinatra – bending notes was associated with blues and African American singers such as Billie Holiday – and directed him to operate as a subtle ethnomusicologist. Based on the apparition of the object of affection on a bedroom ceiling, the last verse of Sinatra's 'Dancing on the Ceiling', from his first torch ballad LP *In the Wee Small Hours* (1955), takes note-bending to its furthest extreme, contorting the last word of one phrase upwards until it becomes the first word of the next phrase. More exaggerated than in 'One for My Baby (and One More for the Road)', the glissando effect reinforces the otherworldly narrative structuring the song. 'You must look at the lyric, and understand it,' Sinatra commented, since 'the word actually dictates to you in a song – it really tells you what it needs.'[8] Bending a note at any other point in 'Dancing on the Ceiling' would not have optimized the lyric to the same degree.

While vocally Holiday influenced Sinatra, by the the 1950s the dynamic between the two was reciprocal. Sinatra's torch ballad LPs of the 1950s substantially informed one of Holiday's last LPs, *Lady in Satin* (1958). From Sinatra's *In the Wee Small Hours*, Holiday includes 'I Get Along without You Very Well', 'Glad to Be Unhappy' and 'I'll Be Around'; from *Where Are You?*, 'I'm a Fool to Want You'; and from *Close to You* (1957), 'It's Easy to Remember' and 'The End of a Love Affair'. Although Holiday was the same age as Sinatra, her voice is reduced to a parched croak on *Lady in Satin*, the consequence of hard knocks and hard living, as Sinatra's would be two decades later on *She Shot Me Down* (1981). When Holiday attempts to bend a note in *Lady in Satin*, it cracks. Musicians such as Holiday's favoured accompanist, Lester Young, doffed their hats in Sinatra's direction, and using his customary profanity, Miles Davis, who Sinatra was

Billie Holiday performing live in her prime during the 1940s.

rumoured to be making a collaborative LP with in the early 1960s following *Sketches of Spain* (1960), called Sinatra's phrasing – like anything he found to be felicitous – a 'motherfucker'.[9]

The continual vocal exchange between Holiday and Sinatra high-lights how the crooner generates a space – both an actual one, in the nightclubs of Harlem and 52nd Street, where they met and inter-acted, and a more intangible one, in the culture at large – beyond

gender and racial differences, in which dialogue between musicians takes place in environments less restricted by the social barriers of the time. As a second-generation Italian immigrant, Sinatra campaigned tirelessly for ethnic minorities, from playing the lead in the short propaganda film *The House I Live In* (1945), released to combat mounting antisemitism at the end of the Second World War onwards, to insisting that singers whose surnames end in a vowel proudly retain their given names – resisting early pressures to change his own name to Frankie Satin – and that African American performers be afforded equal rights in the nightclubs and casinos they appeared in. In this way, the emotional intelligence driving Sinatra's vocal performances navigated him through the complex social issues of the time, including Martin Luther King Jr's freedom marches, which Sinatra supported by appearing at benefit concerts. A catalyst for both aesthetic and social change, Sinatra's music ran parallel with the progressive political causes that he supported from the late 1930s to the mid-1960s.

While not personally close to Holiday, Sinatra did continually assist another African American singer, Sammy Davis Jr. Besides insisting that Davis receive the same treatment as white entertainers, Sinatra advised the younger singer on vocal approach. So important was this to Davis that an affectionate impersonation of Sinatra's torch-ballad singing style was featured in the younger singer's nightclub act from the late 1950s onwards. 'I'd been playing around with an impression of him,' Davis recounts, '[and] watching him all the time I was able to catch the physical things he does, his hands, his mouth, and his shoulders, as well as the voice.'[10] Wearing a trilby and dragging on a cigarette, Davis sings the opening verse of 'One for My Baby (and One More for the Road)', the single spotlight picking him out, aping Sinatra's live performance of the song. The way Davis perfected each of Sinatra's vocal mannerisms – especially

Sinatra and Sammy Davis Jr appearing on a TV show together in the mid-1960s.

note bending – clearly signals the identity of the figure being impersonated. Tellingly, the only thing missing is the gravity of emotion, Davis's myriad abilities lending themselves more to vaude-ville than straightforward emotive crooning. This makes it all the more intriguing that Davis was able to expertly pull off a version of 'Lush Life' on *The Wham of Sam* (1961) – released on Sinatra's fledg-ling Reprise label – just three years after Sinatra's failed attempt to include it on *Only the Lonely*.

The third track on Side 1 of *Only the Lonely*, 'What's New?', presses all four of the above vocal techniques – sustaining, fullness, enunciation and bending – with all of their sonic and sociological complexities, into the service of interpretation. The results of the combination are nothing less than a peerless example of modern crooning. 'What's New?' simply bristles with emotion. Telling the story of one side of a chance encounter with a former lover, the lyrics centre on a hurt character, who doesn't even have the where-withal to drown his sorrows with drink as on 'One for My Baby (and One More for the Road)'. While Sinatra's voice is at the centre of the stereo imaging, Riddle's orchestration provides an apt setting for it, contributing to the cinematic quality of *Only the Lonely*. 'To me a score for a vocalist to sing a song is like the soundtrack to some film sequence,' says Riddle, and 'if the lyrics don't conjure up this picture on their own, I think deeply about the melody and let it supply the picture . . . [so that] my arrangement becomes a comple-ment to this sort of mental film sequence.'[11] Glutted with emotion but never to the point of being cloying, the back and forth between the voice and the arrangement throughout *Only the Lonely* produces an incredibly rich sonic textile. In terms of the economy of the collaboration with Sinatra, Riddle recounts:

> The way we'd work is this: [Sinatra would] pick out all the
> songs for an album and then call me over to go through them.
> He'd have very definite ideas about the general treatment,

particularly about the pace of the record and which areas should be soft or loud, happy or sad. He'd sketch out something brief like, 'Start with a bass figure, build up second time through and then fade out at the end.' That's possibly all he would say. Sometimes he'd follow this up with a phone call at three in the morning with some other extra little idea. But after that he wouldn't hear my arrangement until the recording session.[12]

Employing a large cast of 38 session musicians conducted by Riddle – with violinist Felix Slatkin leading the string section, and augmented by Bill Miller on piano – Sinatra reads the introspective verses of 'What's New?' in an almost conversational manner, as if talking directly to a previous lover. The opening lyrical salvo comes in the form of a question implicit to the song's title. The next verse follows the same pattern. Sinatra's perfect enunciation means each word can be clearly heard and understood, realizing the lyrics' full narrative potential as the song essays the narrator's vulnerability. Against these quietly spoken verses, the emotional release of the title phrase 'What's New?' finds Sinatra singing in almost operatic voice, belting out the phrase and sustaining it over a number of bars. Piercing through the gloom, the fullness of voice achieved here is so exaggerated it takes on a three-dimensional character as it seems to jump out from the speakers. As if that wasn't enough vocal dynamism for one track, in full voice Sinatra then bends the last syllable of the title phrase upwards to link with the first word of the next verse. An instrumental passage follows in which a trombone played by Ray Sims sobs its way through a solo. Then Sinatra re-enters, seemingly exhausted by the loud emotional outburst of the title phrase, able to only manage an additional, pathetic comment about it being nice to see the previous lover again. Pushing the limits of the interpretation of a lyric, read in an even quieter manner than the previous verses – almost in *sotto voce* – the line serves to emphasize the emotional state of the narrator. A final powerful belt of the title phrase finds the narrator gathering himself for one last outburst and concludes with a line in which the protagonist declares his enduring love for the woman being addressed. Listening to Sinatra's vocal performance is an enthralling experience, but it's also exhausting. 'What's New?' is nothing less than a penetrating assault on moderate emotional ground, forcing the listener to embrace an emotional extreme.

The relationship Sinatra established with the studio team is fundamental to the sound of his recorded vocals on 'What's New?'. Once cut using a two-track machine, a playback of the best take of the track followed, with Sinatra and Cavanaugh either approving or disapproving of the selection as a final master. The playback provided the opportunity to listen and identify any necessary coloration on the track, such as the addition of echo, taking place in the control booth in dialogue with the engineer. Keeping the slates – the producer announcing 'Master 19257, Take One' – the session reels of the final masters for each track were then spliced together to form the complete *Only the Lonely* master reference disc, subsequently taken away and listened to in its entirety by Sinatra and Cavanaugh. Once approved by both singer and producer, the identifying slates were removed and the master tape of *Only the Lonely* was made.

Artifice is essential to the crooner's effective performance of a torch ballad. By optimizing his vocal apparatus on 'What's New?', Sinatra pushes the voice as instrument to such an extreme that his performance momentarily blurs the line between person and character. Playing on the ambiguity between the two by inhabiting the character portrayed in a song in the same way he would a character in a film, Sinatra carefully acts out each phrase of the lyric 'what's new?' But no degree of artifice can make up for a lack of emotional intelligence, a quality Sinatra had in abundance. According to Riddle, Sinatra's key collaborator on *Only the Lonely*, the singer's emotional life – with a failed marriage to actress Ava Gardner leading to an emotional breakdown and his attempted suicide in 1951 – deeply informed the singer's ability to infuse the torch ballad with feeling. 'Ava taught him how to sing a torch song,' insists Riddle, 'she taught him the hard way.'[13] Keenly aware of this, Sinatra referred to himself as an '18-karat manic depressive'.[14] Channelling it through a keen sense of artifice, Sinatra controls the depth and degree of emotional impact delivered by his vocal performance.

Rather than parlaying with camp and exploring a broader approach to masculinity, as would be the case with numerous subsequent crooners from Scott Walker and Bryan Ferry onwards, Sinatra's manipulation of the artifice of crooning is underpinned by a very different type of masculinity. 'The swaggering resonance' of Sinatra's voice, writes Tracy Thorn in *Naked at the Albert Hall* (2016), 'brings with it a sense of innate machismo'.[15] While Thorn is surely referring to Sinatra's more upbeat songs, typified by the Cahn and Van Heusen-penned 'Come Fly with Me', released in the same year as *Only the Lonely*, torch ballads like 'What's New?' are simply the other side of the same coin, emphasizing the wounded man instead of the swinger. This may explain why Sinatra was unable to cut 'Lush Life' that evening in 1958 for *Only the Lonely*: perhaps the lyrics, which also included a reference to 'gay places', were too camp.[16] But this is unlikely, since Sinatra befriended the queer actors Montgomery Clift in 1953 and Laurence Harvey in 1962 and attempted to poach gay composer and lyricist Billy Strayhorn from Duke Ellington in 1962. In 'Notes on Camp' (1964), Susan Sontag writes of how camp taste 'consists in going against the grain of one's sex'.[17] In his conducting of Peggy Lee's LP of romantic ballads *The Man I Love* (1957), just prior to cutting *Only the Lonely*, Sinatra demonstrates a capability for exploring the same emotional dynamics from the point of view of the female subject, belying a seldom-acknowledged complexity to his emotional make-up.

Seeking the freedom to find new settings for his voice, following the release of *Only the Lonely*, Sinatra's frustrations with Capitol grew, and he attempted to buy a record label. Initially negotiating to acquire Verve, famous for its LPs with vocalists such as Holiday and Ella Fitzgerald, instead Sinatra started a new, independent, LA-based label, Reprise Records, in 1960.[18] The label was conceived to be swing based and pro-artist, with each musician – including Ben Webster, Rosemary Clooney, Duke Ellington and Sammy Davis Jr – retaining ownership of their masters and being free to record with other labels. Following the founding of Apple Records by the Beatles later in the same decade, artist-run labels would become more common. But in 1960, owning your own label was a strident thing for an artist to do. Johnny Mandel, who arranged Sinatra's first LP, *Ring a Ding Ding!* (1961), on the fledgling label recalls how his intention was to implement new ideas, like the use of coloured vinyl: "'[The pressings] were all going to be different colours," [Sinatra] said. And everybody's going to own their own masters . . . I remember just watching his eyes as he was talking about the company, you know, and they were sparkling.'[19] Owning and operating a label was key to the plans Sinatra had for the new decade, which included working with a wider pool of arrangers and moving within different idioms; cutting harder swinging jazz with Count Basie and Duke Ellington; and putting out LPs of rhythm and blues, bossa nova and folk rock while continuing to release collections of torch ballads. Following a studio visit by George Harrison to one of Sinatra's recording sessions in autumn 1968, an LP devoted to songs composed specifically for him by the Beatle was even rumoured.

Another way Sinatra used Reprise to maintain a footing in contemporary popular music was by exploring the dynamic between the spoken and the sung word in the contexts of soft rock and pop. As Eisenhower's 'man in the grey flannel suit' of the 1950s gave way to John F. Kennedy's 'New Frontier' of the early 1960s, Sinatra remained a vital part of contemporary mainstream popular music, but once Lyndon B. Johnson was in office, and the British Beat invasion of 1964 took hold, Sinatra and contemporary popular tastes began to part company – a distance that was intensified by his support of Nixon's conduct of the Vietnam War from 1968 onwards. In response to the era of The Who's *Tommy* (1969), Sinatra recorded more overt concept LPS. At their most inventive, the Reprise LPS of the late 1960s find Sinatra using his voice to respond to contemporary developments in popular music, not by aping them but by translating the passage of his idiom – swing music and torch ballads – into the music of the time. Despite this effort, the feeling of a figure from an earlier generation moving out of sync with the times is acute on Sinatra's concept LP *A Man Alone* (1969). Even though the singer piloted the proto-concept LP in the 1950s, with the market's shift in emphasis from the single to the LP a decade later, Sinatra's greatest commercial success was, conversely, in the singles market, with upbeat releases such as 'Strangers in the Night' (1966), 'That's Life' (1966) and 'My Way' (1969). The whiff of desperation emanating from Sinatra's concept LPS from the late 1960s is eminently palpable but makes for intriguing listening.

A suite of torch ballads composed by populist poet and songwriter Rod McKuen and arranged by Don Costa – who replaced Riddle as Sinatra's preferred arranger in the late 1960s – *A Man Alone* was conceived with Sinatra's even deeper, now cello-like, voice in mind. 'I had tried for years to reach Frank; wrote songs with him in mind, but could never get to him,' says McKuen, but 'when we finally met, instead of just offering to do just one or two [of my songs], he promised me an entire album, which he'd never done before for any other composer.'[20] Composed of six songs and five spoken-word segments, *A Man Alone* is Sinatra's only collection devoted to the torch ballad from the late 1960s, a period of his output that remains overlooked. Parodying the pathos of *Only the Lonely* with its spoken-word segments, *A Man Alone* frequently slides into bathos, with the poems finding Sinatra dropping the perfect diction of his singing voice in favour of the habitual New Jersey accent of his spoken voice. Not as flexible as it was a decade earlier, and with its ability to sustain and bend a note vastly reduced, Sinatra's voice became more reliant on fullness and perfect enunciation than ever at this point.[21]

For an individual known for his singing voice to feature the spoken one so heavily on a record is highly unusual. On *A Man Alone*, the capability of the singing voice to eradicate place and the speaking voice to reveal it is compelling. Further pursued by Barry White in the early 1970s, the potential role of the spoken voice in the torch ballad would only be fully realized with hip hop in the 1990s, on tracks such as 'Miss U' (1997) by the Notorious B.I.G and 'Bye Baby' (2012) by Nas. Bonz Malone's article 'O.G.: Frank Sinatra Didn't Take Orders; He Took Over' highlights the importance of Sinatra's torch ballad LPs such as *Only the Lonely* for hip hop, commenting on the almost-spoken verses of the final track: 'For the poor schmuck whose wife got tired and left him,' Malone writes, '[Sinatra] kicks "One for My Baby (and One More for the Road)".'[22] Less well known than the Johnny Mercer song, the spoken-word sections of *A Man Alone* would have added further ballast to Malone's argument.

Using devices culled from hip hop and Holiday in equal measure, an offcut from Amy Winehouse's debut LP *Frank* (2003), 'Half Time', pays homage to Sinatra's voice on his torch ballads, with a lyric that describes how singing like him emotionally pacifies the artist. In paying homage to Sinatra, Winehouse retools Holiday's vocal inflections via hip hop, the bending of notes from the 1930s accentuated using the staccato rhythms of the 1990s. If Sinatra was unable to pacify a wider cultural ache by producing an LP of torch ballads in the same style – and scaling the same heights – as *Only the Lonely* again after 1958, then he was not alone: nor was anyone else. The way forward for the crooner was to infiltrate other genres by translating these motifs and tendencies in ways Sinatra could not have imagined.

2

Scott Walker: 'It's Raining Today' (1969)

Scott was static when he recorded a vocal [in the studio].
I don't remember him doing any actions or facial expressions
other than what was required just to get the sound down . . .
all his emotion and all his intent came from his voice.[1]

Early in 1969 at Philips's Marble Arch studios in West London, Scott Walker brazenly departed from the style of crooning that Frank Sinatra piloted in the previous decade. The sensibility of the phlegmatic Belgian Jacques Brel guides Walker in rejecting the sun of Sinatra's Los Angeles – where later crooners as various as Barry White and Tom Waits would also locate themselves – in favour of the existential grey of post-war Europe. Despite this, the smooth baritone Walker uses in the 1960s contrasts sharply with the coarseness of Brel's, its honeyed tone being closer in character to the likes of u.s.-based Sinatra copyists like Jack Jones and Andy Williams. Tellingly, Walker's first two solo LPs devote almost the same amount of space to popular contemporary torch ballads associated with Jones and Williams as to songs by the Belgian chansonnier. Blending aspects of the 1950s sensibilities of both the United States and Europe, a third component, in the form of self-penned songs such as 'Montague Terrace (in Blue)' (1967), constitutes the most vital part of Walker's first two solo LPs and beyond. Dwarfing the cover versions, these self-penned songs create an entirely new model for the crooner by dramatically refashioning the torch ballad and its delivery. On these tracks, Walker's voice is at its most dynamic. '[Scott's] voice has become a simile', writes Marc

Almond in the liner notes for a retrospective collection of Walker's self-penned songs, 'for all crooning, deep tones and liquid vibrato.'[2] Previously crooners just selected their material and its treatment by the arranger, but from Walker onwards, they pen their own songs too. The creative remit of the crooner was widening, albeit without relinquishing the incredible vocal ability associated with past figures such as Sinatra.

Arranged by Phil Spector collaborator Jack Nitzsche, Walker's first vocal vehicle was the track 'Love Her' (1965) with The Walker Brothers. Johnny Franz produced the trio's following records at Philips's Marble Arch studios in close partnership with engineer Peter Olliff, with Walker recalling how both had been arranging and producing Dusty Springfield's music but Olliff couldn't quite get the Spector-like Wall Of Sound Walker was looking for.[3] 'I knew what was happening at the bottom end,' says Walker, referencing his previous experiences as a bass player, 'and that's what made it complete.'[4] Operating alongside Olliff was another engineer, Roger Wake, who worked specifically on capturing suitable vocal takes. 'People like Scott and Dusty . . . were so similar in that they were so particular about their vocals: they had to be "perfect",' Wake recalls, '[and] if they felt they hadn't sung something properly – even if it sounded perfect to everybody else – we'd have to do it again.'[5] Where Sinatra sang live with the orchestra, even when multi-track recording became the norm in the mid-1960s, Walker tended to do his vocals in isolation. Together with arranger Ivor Raymonde, this team was responsible for The Walker Brothers singles 'Make It Easy on Yourself' (1965) and 'The Sun Ain't Gonna Shine Anymore' (1966). With both recordings, the trio's interpretations stay conservatively close to the originals by Jerry Butler and Frankie Valli, with additional reverb courtesy of Philips's echo chamber being the only noticeable difference. This reliance on existing material – and the tendency to adhere to previous interpretations of it – introduces a fault line that only widens with Walker's solo career.

Due to the lack of availability of an alternative model in contemporary popular music, following the disbanding of The Walker Brothers in early 1967, Walker continued to rely heavily on existing material by contemporary songwriters. As of Spring 1967, no other prominent singer had entered the public eye as a member of a group and then left to forge a successful solo career. A year later, and Walker's transition to a solo artist would surely have been eased by the examples set in 1968 by Neil Young in LA after leaving Buffalo Springfield and Syd Barrett in London exiting Pink Floyd. With no such precedent available in 1967, Walker was, you sense, forced to compromise when putting together *Scott* (1967) and *Scott 2* (1968) by relying on a hybrid of existing models of the long player instead of fashioning a new one. With their carefully crafted lyrics, Brel's songs certainly provide a fitting context for Walker's self-penned material, but the covers of contemporary popular tunes associated with Jones and Williams, typified by Burt Bacharach's 'Windows of the World', feel like filler, weakening the first two solo LPs considerably. Walker also permitted Philips to create themes for subsequent recordings made of other writers' material in the same manner as Columbia and Capitol would with Jones and Williams, with *Scott Walker Sings Songs from His TV Series* being released later in 1969 and *The Moviegoer* following three years later. The upshot of these compromises was that despite leaning towards Europe in this period, the young Walker would never completely escape the undertow of the U.S. Sinatra copyist.

'People were winding me up,' Walker recalls of this time, 'saying, "You can be the next Sinatra."'[6] Although closer to Jones and Williams than to Sinatra in vocal tone, Walker was understandably more drawn to Sinatra. 'I am working on my own, studying breath control and phrasing,' Walker explained in 1966, '[but] I'd like to be able to put that styling into a song [as] Sinatra does in "A Very Good Year".'[7] What is so innovative about 'It Was a Very Good Year' is the way Sinatra takes what is essentially an early 1960s folk song – as

Brel in the early 1960s recording the song 'Domino'.

Sinatra referred to it in live performances – narrating the story of a man's life, and sets it to the type of orchestral arrangement associated with a torch ballad from the previous decade. The result is a more reflective contemporary Sinatra that sounded relatively fresh in 1965 at the time of its release on the LP *September of My Years*. Because of the way it uses both newer material and instrumentation in a gambit for a totally contemporary sound, another of Sinatra's mid-1960s LPS, *Strangers in the Night* (1966), triggered derision from Walker. 'Sinatra degrades himself by doing this rubbish,' spits Walker in response to the LP's admittedly ersatz title track, '[and] the phrasing, at which Sinatra normally excels, sounds like a train labouring uphill.'[8] During the Walker Brothers' live shows, Walker would often sing the Bacharach song off-stage and their drummer, Gary Walker, would mime to it, eyes screwed up in mock emotion. A further track from Sinatra's *Strangers in the Night* LP came in for even harsher criticism. 'Listening to [Sinatra] doing numbers like "Downtown", comments Walker referring to a version of Petula Clark's signature song, 'is like watching an old man trying to jive.'[9] With the aim of providing stronger contemporary material, a few years later Walker even considered writing songs for Sinatra. 'I'd like to be able to get in a position that Rod McKuen was in with that *Man Alone* album for Sinatra,' Walker commented after hearing the 1969 LP solely composed for the singer by the songwriter and poet.[10] Humorously, when organizing the Meltdown Festival in 1999, Nick Cave asked Walker to sing 'My Way' as part of his brief set. Walker declined.

'I'm obsessed by those things that are ugly or sordid that people don't want to talk about as if they were afraid of touching a wound,' Brel declared.[11] This is the essential element differentiating the Belgian chansonnier's songwriting from the composers of the so-called Great American Songbook of the 1930–50s drawn on by Sinatra. 'When I first heard Brel,' Walker says, 'it showed me that it could be done. I'd never heard anyone else who could write like that.'[12] Brel contrasts sharply with not only these historical figures but then-current progressive American contemporary songwriters – including, to Walker's mind, Bob Dylan.[13] Released by the same record label that Walker was on, Philips, the Brel LPs available in the UK in 1967 included *La Valse à mille temps* (1959), *Enregistrement public à l'Olympia 1964* and *Ces gens-là* (1966), containing 'My Death', 'Amsterdam' and 'Mathilde', all covered on *Scott*.

> What you have . . . is the enthusiasm of . . . me finding the work and wanting to get in the studio as quickly as possible and cut 'em live. I got those translations and set up those sessions as fast as I could, and that energy is probably what comes across.[14]

Yielding positive results when carefully filtered into Walker's own writing, the widely celebrated Brel covers rapidly recorded for *Scott* and then for *Scott 2* and *Scott 3* (1969) tend to be overly theatrical, with contemporaneous covers by Dusty Springfield and Nina Simone faring much better. The problem turns on how Walker transforms Brel's songs into show tunes, polishing guttural abjection into a burlesque sheen. Compare versions of the torch song 'If You Go Away' from *Scott 3* with 'Ne me quitte pas' from *La Valse à mille temps* (1959). Brel's recording is relatively sparse and the more effective for it, simply voicing the impassioned lyric. A later version from the LP *Ne me quitte pas* (1972) on Barclay Records, with Brel's vocal tones having darkened in the intermittent period, is even more effective. With its exaggerated drama, Walker's 'If You Go Away' turns the song into something from a Stephen Sondheim musical, a close cousin of 'Send in the Clowns'.

By turning pathos into bathos so insistently, Walker's Brel cover versions are emphatically camp. 'The sensibility of failed seriousness', writes Susan Sontag in 'Notes on Camp' (1966), a year before Walker's first Brel cover, opens out onto what she terms 'the theatricalization of experience'.[15] When theatricalized in this way by Walker, the ribald nature of Brel's lyrics is cancelled out. Walker's tendency towards a limp sense of camp both with the Brel interpretations and the constant references to intellectuals such as Albert Camus and Ingmar Bergman finds him channelling the historical figure of the dandy. 'As the dandy is the 19th century's surrogate for the aristocrat in matters of culture,' expands Sontag, 'so Camp is the modern dandyism.'[16] Appropriately, Walker often wore a velvet jacket for concerts and TV appearances during the late 1960s, as if in homage to the archetypical figure of the historical dandy, Oscar Wilde. While Walker's tendency towards camp saps the potency out of Brel's lyrics, it does have the benefit of making the chansonnier's songs available to later generations. Drawn to Brel by Walker's example, David Bowie's versions of 'My Death' and 'Amsterdam'

American singer-songwriter Scott Walker seen during a guest appearance, 11 March 1969, on *Mr and Mrs Music* – a programme based around songwriting husband and wife duo Tony Hatch and Jackie Trent.

from the early 1970s come off better for being sung in the guise of Ziggy Stardust, the fictitious character dealing effectively with the inherent theatricality of the lyrics.[17] Marc Almond's later reading of Brel songs on *Jacques* (1989) take a different tact, pushing back at Walker's interpretations by finding a way to recover the macabre quality of Brel's lyrics.[18]

French singer Charles Aznavour in 1973.

Fortunately, Walker's fascination with Brel soon lessened. 'Brel is a lyric writer,' explains Walker in 1969, but 'he doesn't write good melodies, and because I am now just as concerned with the music as well as lyrics, it is impossible for me to record any more of Brel's material.'[19] None of the chansonnier's songs are included on Walker's subsequent LPs, *Scott 4* (1969) and *'Til the Band Comes In* (1970). Not revered by Walker the way Brel and Sinatra were, their contemporary Charles Aznavour was a figure in the French chanson tradition with a keen ability to place an equal emphasis on melody and lyrics, combining the vocal qualities of the crooner of the 1950s with the songwriting abilities of the singer-songwriter of the 1960s. Less aggressive than Brel's, Aznavour's lyrics tend to empathize with, rather than just observe, characters and situations. Composed at a later date, 'What Makes a Man a Man' from the LP *Idiote je t'aime* (1972) finds Aznavour inhabiting the character of a man working as a transvestite striptease artist. The sense of the transvestite being an outsider is perfectly captured in Aznavour's lyric. Although Scott chose to only cover one Aznavour song, 'Who (Will Take My Place)' on *Scott Walker Sings Songs from His TV Series*, Aznavour, with his gift for melody, could easily have replaced Brel as an appropriate guiding influence on Walker in 1969. The self-penned song 'Big Louise' from *Scott 3* is described by Walker as nothing less than 'a requiem for an aging homosexual'.[20] Besides numerous Brel songs, it's no coincidence that Almond has covered both Aznavour's 'What Makes a Man a Man' and Walker's 'Big Louise', the latter on the first Marc and the Mambas LP (1982).

Walker's turn away from Brel also marks his complete immersion in songwriting, a key aspect of an artist's currency in the late 1960s. Partly influenced by Dylan rather than Brel, bands such as the Kinks and the Beatles had been crafting LPs consisting entirely of self-penned songs since as early as 1964. For an LP by a leading pop act, *Scott* (1967) lags behind them, as it includes only three self-penned songs, the remaining nine tracks being split between covers of popular songs and those by Brel. *Scott 2* (1968) repeats the formula. Though overshadowed by its successor, Walker's next LP, *Scott 3*, marked a breakthrough since it dropped the cover versions of popular material to make way for ten self-penned songs – the same amount as on the widely celebrated *Scott 4*. Walker refers to the self-penned material as being 'like surrealistic songs done in orchestral movement'.[21]

In 1968, when Walker began recording *Scott 3*, the status of the LP was very different to when Sinatra's *Only the Lonely* was recorded a decade earlier. By now the concept LP was being developed on a wider front in terms of both its conceptualization and execution. In LA and London, artists from the Beach Boys to the Kinks developed myriad approaches to the concept LP, the Kinks having produced a succession of them from 1967 to 1970, concluding with *Lola Versus Powerman and the Moneygoround, Part One* (1970) and its title song narrating the actions of a transexual. Instead of launching his solo career in 1967 with a 7″ single, as was common practice, Walker went straight to the LP. 'I'm cutting an LP before a single,' Walker explained of *Scott*, 'because an album will give me more room to develop a new kind of style.'[22] While *Scott 2* repeats the formula of the first LP, *Scott 3* is more focused, being devoted to, in Walker's words, 'songs of love and loneliness'.[23] Alternating between obtuse love songs such as 'Copenhagen' and 'Butterfly', the torch songs 'It's Raining Today' and 'Two Weeks Since You've Gone', and commentaries on figures of loneliness with 'Big Louise' and 'Rosemary', *Scott 3* is arguably Walker's most effective LP.

Extending Walker's 'surrealistic songs done in orchestral movement', the LP following *Scott 4*, *'Til the Band Comes In*, started out as an even more fully articulated concept LP, converging around eccentric characters living in the same tenement block. The instrumental 'Prologue' opening the LP begins with the sound effects of a tap dripping, children playing, a door slamming and assorted adult voices. Each of the songs on Side 1 and the first half of Side 2 offers a vignette of a different character from the tenement block: 'Joe' narrates the story of an old man who dies unnoticed in his flat; 'Thanks for Chicago Mr James' captures a cowboy writing a kiss-off letter (a letter or song which celebrates the end of a relationship) to his keeper; 'Time Operator' replays a conversation between a lonely man and the talking clock; 'Jean the Machine' the nocturnal activities of a stripper, and 'Cowbells Shakin'' the passions of an immigrant waiter. Unfortunately, this is as far as the concept goes on the LP, and the remaining space on Side 2 is given over to filler in the form of covers of contemporary popular songs as per Walker's first two solo records. If Walker had pursued this direction on subsequent LPS the results would have made for intriguing listening.

Crucial to the maturation of the concept LP was the use of the studio as a tool in recording. In 1966 in LA the Byrds released *Fifth Dimension*, while in London the Beatles completed *Revolver*. Studio technology previously rendered relatively transparent by producers now became increasingly opaque. Technology overtly infiltrated not only the recording process but the writing process, the two becoming entwined, especially on tracks such as the Byrds' 'Eight Miles High' and the Beatles' 'I'm Only Sleeping', with the use of drone guitar by David Crosby and backwards guitar by Paul McCartney, respectively. By 1969 the role of the studio was enhanced as vocals were subject to myriad types of manipulation. Walker's voice on the chorus of 'The Amorous Humphrey Plugg' from *Scott 2* is treated using a pronounced 'flanging' effect – the playing of two versions of a vocal track at slightly different speeds – as piloted by Les Paul in the late 1940s and used to great effect by mixing engineer Larry Levine on Toni Fisher's version of 'The Big Hurt' (1959). In 1968 Walker opted to become more embroiled in the recording process by producing two jazz LPS for Philips: guitarist Terry Smith's *Fallout* (1969) and saxophonist Ray Warleigh's *The Ray Warleigh Album* (1969), both of whom joined Ronnie Scott in backing Walker in live concerts of the period. Following these experiences, Walker's understanding of the role of the studio in recording increased accordingly. '[Arranging is] not an easy thing to do, because it's not a visual thing,' explains Walker, since 'we can storyboard the movie . . . we can draw pictures of what it should look like frame by frame, and people can see that – but not with music.'[24] Using an eight-track recording console, with *Scott 3* Walker and producer Franz refrain from emphasizing studio trickery. The result is a more subtle use of the contemporary studio as a tool for the crooner.

While benefitting from aspects of the use of the studio and the formulation of the LP by rock and pop acts from the late 1960s, Walker remains at one remove. '[Walker] was not part of the underground scene,' affirms Barry Miles, editor of the *International Times*, being instead 'part of the pop world, a very different thing'.[25] Walker actively distanced himself from both the underground and the rock scene in numerous ways but principally by turning down a management offer from Brian Epstein and opting to play theatres and social clubs instead of larger rock venues such as the Roundhouse.[26] Rolling Stones manager Andrew Loog Oldham and business partner Tony Calder were intrigued by Walker and initially considered working with him too. 'Andrew and I started to focus on Scott,' Calder recalls, shrewdly observing how 'we were looking at a future mega solo nightclub star, Jacques Brel-cum-Boddy Darin a la Frank Sinatra,' rather than a figure operating within the context of rock.[27] Tellingly, of the countless London-based musicians included in the Beatles' 'All You Need Is Love' global satellite TV broadcast shot in June 1967 – including Mick Jagger, Marianne Faithfull, Eric Clapton and Keith Moon – it was John Walker of The Walker Brothers and not Scott who attended and is visible in the footage.

If the impetus to write songs using penetrating lyrics is initially triggered by listening to Brel, then Walker's ideas for the arrangements commissioned to accompany them has no real precedent in popular music. Describing them as 'like surrealistic songs done in orchestral movement' could not have been more apt.[28] Much of this orchestral colour comes from modern European composers whom Walker was enthralled by such as Jean Sibelius, Anton Webern and Alban Berg. '[Scott] was always quoting symphonies to me: "I want it like Sibelius' Seventh Symphony",' recalls one of Walker's most frequent arrangers, Wally Stott.[29] Where 'We Came Through' from

Scott 3 channels the dissonant brass of Sibelius, 'Big Louise' taps into the abstraction of Webern. 'Classical composers have made huge leaps,' says Walker in 1968 of modern composers, 'but have progressed without becoming unmusical.'[30] Certainly, the arrangements on Walker's self-penned songs are experimental but retain enough melody and structure to work within the idiom of the three-to-four-minute pop song. While Nelson Riddle introduced Debussy-like touches on Sinatra's *Only the Lonely* (1958), Walker and Stott take the modern orchestral sensibility to an entirely new level. Stott's co-arranger Keith Roberts describes the process by which Walker's arrangements were arrived at: 'I would be presented beforehand with a demo . . . [with] just him singing and playing guitar,' Roberts says, 'but you'd also have some . . . chord symbols, and the words, the melody line and the harmony on top.'[31] Roberts was unusually sensitive to Walker's lyrics. 'The words were very important to me as an arranger,' Roberts explains, 'I'd accentuate a certain lyric with a timpani, for instance . . . On a [certain] song, I wouldn't have powerful trumpets going; you'd have blended strings and delicate instruments.'[32] Once the arrangement had been shaped, one of Philips's studios would be booked. 'Scott would be listening in the control room, or he might come out to the studio to listen,' continues Roberts, '[and] he might even have stood next to the conductor. You'd have a few rehearsals first . . . [and] then you'd rectify those and do a take.'[33] The initial guide vocal would then be replaced by the definitive one recorded at a later date.

Walker turns to a diverse array of sources for lyrical content, but one constant is European film, especially the British kitchen sink dramas of the late 1950s and early 1960s and Ealing comedies of the late 1940s and 1950s. Even prior to the relocation to London in 1965, Walker was intrigued by both. 'I'd been watching Ealing comedies and people like Margaret Rutherford and Terry Thomas,' explains Walker, 'and when I got [to London] I thought it's not going to be the same. But we arrived in the Winter and it was really bleak and there were those kinds of people running around.'[34] Walker was surprised by how conversations about cinema in the UK always turned towards films made in the place Walker relocated from: LA. Narrative devices from both genres of British cinema infiltrate Walker's lyrics, beginning with the 1966 EP track 'Mrs Murphy' which focuses on the inhabitants of a tenement flat. The central character from 'The Amorous Humphrey Plugg' (1968) is equal parts kitchen sink drama and Ealing comedy, with the name 'Plugg' surely having been chosen because it sounds so quintessentially English. After being introduced to Walker via the collection *Fire Escape in the Sky: The God-Like Genius of Scott Walker* compiled by Julian Cope and released by Zoo records in 1981, Marc Almond's band Soft Cell penned 'Kitchen Sink Drama' for their LP *The Art of Falling Apart* (1983).

In terms of vocal tone, perhaps the English balladeer Matt Monro, who came to prominence just before Walker arrived in the UK in 1965 with 'Portrait of My Love' (1961) and 'Softly As I Leave You' (1962), is more relevant than either Sinatra copyists Jack Jones or Andy Williams. With 'From Russia with Love' (1963), Monro deploys that same smooth tone, and such tracks are as much a part of the soundtrack of England in the period as 'The Sun Ain't Gonna Shine Anymore'. Knowing Monro rejected an offer from Sinatra's Reprise records, Capitol decided that Monro would be a suitable replacement for the recently deceased Nat King Cole and signed Monro to the label in 1966, facilitating his relocation to LA.[35] Neither the material Monro chose nor its treatment by producer George Martin – who first signed the singer to Parlophone in 1960 after contracting him to impersonate Sinatra on a Peter Sellers LP – shows any sign of development after these initial tracks in the early 1960s. Like Sinatra copyists Jones and Williams, Monro was unable to develop in terms of song selection or LP conception and soon found himself on the supper and social club circuit.

The opening track on Side 1 of *Scott 3*, 'It's Raining Today', fuses the abstract suspended tonality of Webern with the stark depictive realism of the British kitchen sink drama. The result is incredible. From the opening notes of 'It's Raining Today', the indefinite buzz of the strings provides a high modern backdrop to the scene that lyrically unfolds before it. Walker's voice appears to be laid over the top of the arrangement, revealing the incredible degree of control the singer exerts over his voice, the liquid baritone skimming over the glacial haze of the strings. Seldom does a singer's voice evidence this degree of technical perfection while maintaining such an emotive punch. Closer listening reveals how Walker's voice, along with an acoustic guitar and brushes, occupies the left channel, while the strings buzz and hover in the right. In the three verses of 'It's Raining Today', the narrator describes a vernacular street scene viewed from the vantage point of a series of windows. The first scene refers to a girl viewed through a train window. The window only provides a partial view of the street, being covered with raindrops, its opacity doubled due to the smoke billowing from the narrator's cigarette. The second verse uses the windowpane as a device to recall the past, when the summer heat causes the protagonist to seek shade inside. Dramatically, the kitchen sink drama theme is then introduced in the middle eight, as a context is provided for the shaded rooms referred to in the second verse with the protagonist's bed-sit, owned by an ageing landlady. The final verse then returns to the view of life through the narrator's window, the rain now turning the streets into cellophane. The three seemingly contradictory elements – the arrangement, the lyrics and the voice – are melded together by the way each one finds a technique appropriate to its medium to articulate a sense of stasis: the arrangement using suspended strings, the lyrics describing the rain running down the window, and the voice sustaining the last note of the final word of each phrase. If Walker was anything like the scene described in the opening paragraph, then he too was appropriately static when laying down vocals, recording them in Philips's echo chamber to enhance his liquid vibrato. With its abstract lyrics, 'It's Raining Today' redefines what a torch song consists of. As everything is observed through the opaque pane of glass, the narrator's emotional life is pushed back rather than being brought to the fore. Direct emotion is still present but partially obscured.

Walker was highly sensitized as to the precise timbre and quality of his voice. 'Singing's always hard for me,' Walker admits, 'not physically. But to get it neutral, where it's not too emotional and not too deadpan. Somewhere in between is what I'm looking for.'[36] 'It's Raining Today' walks this tightrope between emotional extremes, with the verses maintaining an even and relatively cool tone only broken in the middle eight. Richard Dodd, an engineer who worked with Walker in the 1970s, recalls two details regarding Walker's preferences for capturing vocal sound:

> [Scott] didn't like anyone to be able to hear him breathe on a record. If you listen to some records, you'll hear that some people use the sound of their breath for emotional effect. Scott would go to great lengths with me to not hear his breath. On the other hand, he would encourage sibilance. He loved it. It's one of those things he's attached to records that he loves and he's associated the anomaly with the reality of the medium ... He'd say, 'Yeah, I want sibilance on my records. And no breath.'[37]

In the mid-1960s Walker was tutored by the Denmark Street vocal coach Freddie Winrose, who, according to Walker, 'greatly increased my range, dexterity and confidence. But most important for me was his way of teaching breath control.'[38] So intense is this breath control, it enables Walker to emphatically emphasize the voice as instrument over the voice as body or character. Sibilance enhances this.

Falling into one of popular music's numerous no man's lands, in the late 1960s Walker was lost somewhere in the transition between the end of the modern and the birth of the postmodern crooner. This shift is most clearly articulated in the contrast between two figures: Sinatra and Bryan Ferry. Where Sinatra consistently develops in a linear fashion in the 1950s and early 1960s by piloting the concept LP and embodying a new vocal approach, in the early 1970s Ferry assembles solo LPs from a collage of existing styles and sounds, temporarily inhabiting each of them before moving on. Caught between the two eras and their associated models of crooning, in the late 1960s Walker struggled to sustain a consistent approach to constructing a repertoire, despite the distinct nature of his self-professed 'surrealistic songs done in orchestral movement'. While The Walker Brothers LPs mostly consist of cover versions, both Walker's first three solo LPs and *'Til the Band Comes In* include covers and self-penned material, while only *Scott 4* is solely devoted to the latter. Add to this the LPs of covers, *Scott Walker Sings Songs from His TV Series* and *The Moviegoer*, and the lack of a distinct approach being sustained becomes more pronounced as time progresses, until the 1980s with Walker's *Climate of Hunter* (1984), when a totally different archetype dominates. By the 1970s, Walker was even allowing Philips's department (responsible for talent scouting and artist development) to totally direct his career. 'If they wanted me to do movie themes, I would pick the best movie themes I thought were possible,' comments Walker, 'and I would do them – Sinatra-type stuff. I'll imitate anybody.'[39] As a result, Walker's optimum period as a crooner spans only three years (1967–9), as opposed to over a decade with Sinatra (1954–69) or Ferry (1972–85). But in those three years, Walker produced some of the most sublime singing ever to be recorded on tape.

3

Barry White:
'Bring Back My Yesterday'
(1973)

T he most exciting part of recording,' says Barry White – sitting in his home studio in Sherman Oaks, Los Angeles – 'is
when you go in and lay the rhythm tracks, and you lay your
percussion tracks, your string tracks, and then you get down to this
board. It either happens here,' White chuckles, 'or it don't.'[1] Once
the appropriate faders on the console have been pushed up and the
separate layers of instrumentation making up the backing track are
revealed, White kicks back and sings in the direction of the camera.
The impression White gives in this brief clip of 16mm footage from
1977 is of an artist controlling every aspect of the recording process
– from songwriting and producing through to arranging and singing
– with apparent ease. White was the only convincing disco crooner.

The ability to transition seamlessly between writing, arranging,
producing and singing sets White aside from not only the previous
two waves of crooners, who either just sang like Sinatra or composed and sang like Scott Walker, but crooners of the future such
as Grace Jones and Nas. However, while having the maximum creative control enabled White to experiment and form a new vocal
topography from 1972 to 1975, the sounding board and safety net
an external producer provides – suggesting new ventures and catch-
ing the singer when they falter – were absent at key moments. To

Barry White (1944–2003), U.S. soul singer, singing into a microphone during a
live concert performance, c. 1975.

put this in context, as the first crooner to own a large label, Reprise Records, Sinatra ran two producers in parallel: Jimmy Bowen for pop singles and Sonny Burke for concept albums. This led to two sharply contrasting types of record, with the former producing 'Something Stupid' (1967) and the latter the first LP with Antônio Carlos Jobim, *Francis Albert Sinatra and Antônio Carlos Jobim*, in the same year. By contrast, White absorbed both roles and formed his own record label, Unlimited Gold, in 1978. The received image of White as purely a slick soundtrack to smooching – the Walrus of Love – tends therefore to elide his ability to simultaneously write, sing and produce with the same degree of ingenuity that a respected popular figure poised between neo-soul and hip hop, such as Pharrell Williams, does today. The crooner as producer, writer and singer was set to be an important part of the development of the archetype.

White cut his teeth in production in LA in the mid-1960s, working for local independent labels such as Mustang/Bronco until an encounter with the vocal trio the Croonettes in 1969. Turning down a lucrative offer to work with the highly successful Motown label, now relocated from Detroit to LA, White signed on as the Croonettes' producer, renamed them Love Unlimited and took the next few years to compose, arrange and produce their debut LP, *From a Girl's Point of View We Give to You . . . Love Unlimited* (1972). Following the LP's success, White searched for a solo male vocalist to interpret a handful of newly written songs. After several fruitless months, White came to an important realization and assumed the role of vocalist as well as producer and songwriter himself.

In shaping a vocal approach, White dialled in to contemporaneous developments made by Marvin Gaye and Isaac Hayes, both of whom gained extensive studio experience in the 1960s at Motown and Stax, respectively, with Gaye's production work with the Originals' running parallel with his high-profile solo career, and Hayes's activity as a songwriter and session musician with Sam and

Black soul singer Isaac Hayes performs at the International Amphitheater in Chicago as part of the annual PUSH (People United to Save Humanity) 'Black Expo' in October 1973.

Dave acting as a precursor to his.[2] Essentially, what Gaye and Hayes did with their flurry of influential LPs in the late 1960s and early 1970s was to gradually transform the acoustic rhythmic elements in Ray Charles's music into fully electrified soft funk. In terms of the development of the torch ballad, Charles is the crucial link between the early 1950s swing of Frank Sinatra – through the 1960s soul of Gaye and then the early 1970s funk of Hayes – and the mid-1970s slow-mo disco funk of White.

The figure Charles in turn drew from early on, and whom Gaye devoted a tribute LP to in 1965 following his death, is Nat King Cole. In the 1940s Cole reserved musical dynamism for his piano playing, the voice serving more as accompaniment, but as the 1950s progressed, every musical nuance displaced between Cole's piano playing and singing became embedded in the voice as it grew in depth and range. Relinquishing the piano altogether by the 1960s, Cole's voice became a remarkably resilient instrument full of texture. Listen to the way Cole sings the word 'cigar' on the Gordon Jenkins-orchestrated track 'Where Did Everyone Go?' (1963), biting down so hard on the word that the customary vocal smoothness is strained and a crack appears, which Cole exploits to emotive ends. The degree of emphasis projects the word forward, forcing it to jump out at the listener.

Often overlooked, there was a constant call and response between Charles and Sinatra between 1959 and 1967, the dialogue serving to propel each singer forward. If 'When Your Lover Has Gone', from *The Genius of Ray Charles* (1959), was triggered by Sinatra's version on *In the Wee Small Hours* (1955), then 'Come Rain or Come Shine' on *Sinatra and Strings* (1962) follows Charles's version that appears on his 1959 LP. More blatantly, in 1964 Sinatra attempted the Charles-associated track 'I Can't Stop Loving You' with Quincy Jones, and Nelson Riddle updated Sinatra's sound using the Hammond organ on 'Summer Wind' (1966), an instrument favoured by Charles during the decade. A year later, Charles doffed the cap in return once more with the string-drenched LP *Ray Charles Invites You to Listen* (1967). The ping-pong between Charles and Sinatra weaves a complexity into the genealogy of the crooner.

Released just two years after his debut LP for Atlantic, *The Genius of Ray Charles* was arguably the key Charles vocal LP for both Gaye and Hayes during their early period of development.[3] Each side of the LP established its own mood: Side 1, typified by the track 'When Your Lover Has Gone', orchestrated by Quincy Jones, was mid- to up-tempo, while Side 2 consisted of string-driven ballads such as 'Come Rain or Come Shine', orchestrated by Ralph Burns. Besides his singing, Charles's unique ability to move between vocal and non-vocal music was crucial for Gaye and Hayes, releasing instrumental LPs such as *Soul Brothers* (1958) and *The Genius After Hours* (1961) either side of *The Genius of Ray Charles*. The way Gaye's largely instrumental soundtrack to the blaxploitation film *Trouble Man* (1972) was bookended by the vocal LPs *What's Going On* (1972) and *Let's Get It On* (1973), and the way Hayes's soundtrack *Shaft* (1971) sandwiched between the vocal-driven *The Isaac Hayes Movement* (1970) and *Black Moses* (1971), would not have been possible without Charles's example. Starting with the nascent funk group Earth, Wind and Fire's soundtrack for *Sweet Sweetback's Baadasssss Song* (1971), the role of the blaxploitation film in offering Hayes and Gaye – and countless others – the opportunity to produce sprawling sequences of mostly non-vocal music, some innovatively incorporating passages of dialogue from the film, is crucial to the development of the ongoing correlation between instrumental and vocal music in the early 1970s. Just as much as it was for Gaye and Hayes, Charles's example was vital for White, who perpetually moved between the vocal-driven work of his solo LPs and those with the Love Unlimited trio, and the purely instrumental output of the Love Unlimited Orchestra. The only time all three of White's parallel ventures are featured together is on the overlooked blaxploitation soundtrack *Together Brothers* (1974).[4]

Containing just four tracks, Hayes's *Hot Buttered Soul* (1969) – the cover proudly filling the 12″ × 12″ of glossy cover space with the singer's bald dome – established a new framework later extended by White's retooling of the crooner archetype, not only in its relaxed mood and use of strings but in its tendency to stretch songs out by using lengthy spoken passages, with 'By the Time I Get to Phoenix' clocking in at a herculean 18 and a half minutes. This interpretation – or, more accurately, complete dismantling – of Jimmy Webb's song actually developed following Hayes's request that Stax regulars the Bar-Keys add the song to their repertoire during a night club residency. Hayes recalls:

> I went on stage, there was a bunch of conversations going in the club, so I told [bass player] James [Alexander] to hold that first chord and sustain it. 'Don't move, don't change, don't do anything.' And I started telling a story about the situation in the song. And the conversations started to subside. Upon the first note of the first verse, I had 'em. And when the song was done, people were crying. I'd touched them.[5]

Hayes used the term 'rap' to refer to this talking intimately with the audience, with tracks on his LPs from 1970 onwards being named and numbered 'Ike's Rap I' and 'Ike's Rap II', later heavily sampled by hip hop crooners such as Nas.[6] The version of 'By the Time I Get to Phoenix' developed during the nightclub residency appearing on *Hot Buttered Soul* stretches the rap out for nearly 9 minutes, when the band eventually relinquish the chord they've been sustaining and move with Hayes into the first verse of the song as written. Since White's first two solo LPs, *I've Got So Much to Give* (1973) and *Stone Gon'* (1973), were comprised of only five tracks a piece, and his third LP, *Can't Get Enough* (1974), included a track that was over 10 minutes in length, Hayes was undoubtedly an important precedent for White's retooling of the crooner archetype. Though doo-wop certainly influenced White's spoken-word raps on his songs, with their extended song length and use of strings, Hayes remains key to understanding White's oeuvre. White's attempts to distance himself from Hayes – defensively commenting that 'he's into his own thing and I'm in mine', but 'I just feel I'm better in mine than he is in his' – were surely spurred by his sensitivity to critics' tendency to unfavourably compare the two, with *Rolling Stone* going so far as to call White an 'imitation Isaac Hayes' when reviewing *Stone Gon'* in 1973.[7]

White was less guarded when it came to Gaye, enthusing about Gaye's ability to fluidly move between roles, with *What's Going On* being a firm favourite.[8] As Gaye's first self-produced concept album, *What's Going On* follows the way Hayes extended tracks using both spoken-word passages and instrumental interludes but injects it with Gil Scott-Heron's contemporaneous tendency towards social commentary developed on both *Small Talk at 125th and Lenox* (1970) and *Pieces of a Man* (1971).[9] Sequences of tracks from *What's Going On* such as 'Save the Children' and 'God Is Love' find Gaye at his most experimental both vocally and instrumentally, smoothly transitioning between traditionally structured verse/chorus segments and spoken-word passages. In light of how White avoided overt politics and social critique, content instead with pridefully embodying African American sensuality, it's curious that his favourite Gaye LP would be the only one overtly produced within the context of the Black Power movement, shot through with poignant commentaries on Vietnam, ecology, urban violence and racial division. Melody and rhythm were perhaps prioritized over lyrical content when White sat down to listen to *What's Going On*.

Initially White appears as if a throwback to the soul era of the early 1960s, when song lyrics focused exclusively on matters pertaining to heterosexual romance, comfortably maintaining the balance between the sentimental and the sensual at the very kernel of traditional crooning. Swing-based crooners including Sinatra and Sammy Davis Jr routinely sensualized what had, by the time they performed it, become relatively sentimental material, such as 'I've Got You Under My Skin'. Soul and funk singers such as Gaye and Hayes frequently adopt the same tactic to interpret material written by others, but when performing their own songs, they veer towards the sensual. White bucks this tendency. By embodying the sensual physically, in terms of the libidinous character of his bass-baritone voice, White lyrically over-emphasizes the sentimental ad nauseum. In defiance of binary readings that privilege one approach over the other, White accesses the sensual precisely through an emphasis on the sentimental.

Released in 1972, the same year as Gaye's vocal follow-up to *What's Going On*, Love Unlimited's 'Walking in the Rain (with the One I Love)' features White's first vocal performance to make it onto long-playing vinyl. With it, White puts listeners on notice as to the vocal delights soon to come on his solo LPs. Influenced by the way doo-wop singles such as the Inkspots' 'I Don't Want to Set the World on Fire' feature a baritone monologue in place of an instrumental break, the final minute of 'Walking in the Rain (with the One I Love)' centres around a spoken-word exchange between White on one end of a telephone and Love Unlimited's Glodean James on the other. 'My engineer fixed the phone so that when I picked it up, it went directly into the twenty-four track,' explains White, and 'I said, "Hello," and then pictured in my mind Glodean saying her part [and] I added, "Did you get caught in the rain?"'[10] The vocal intimacy on which crooning is premised is here deftly extended through the use of the telephone. Despite the low-tech quality of the telephone as a recording device when compared with a studio microphone directly fed into the board, on this 'rap', White's voice still manages to come across as extremely deep and textured.

White describes how his voice came to be in his memoir, *Love Unlimited* (1999): 'When adolescence hit me my sound didn't go down to a tenor, the way most boys do, and stay there, my voice went down *twice*, first to a first tenor and then to a bass singer, that second one like a drop off the Empire State Building.'[11] Until early 1973, White had been content simply with producing and had not considered himself a singer. Listening back to the demo cut of the three new songs featuring his bass-baritone soon changed this. 'It wasn't until I had my producing ears on that I finally "heard" the voice of Barry White. For the first time, I became fully aware of the uniqueness, the powerful romantic pull, the emotional depth of the lure of my own voice.'[12] Vitally, White only came to appreciate the

Barry White and Love Unlimited arrive in London, 3 March 1977.

distinctive qualities of his vocal ability – whether in full singing voice or a spoken rap – through his experience as a producer. This unusual route accounts for White's ability to broaden the archetype of the crooner beyond just the singer and songwriter.

The sonic bed that White's voice would be laid on was crucial. Having originally met him a decade earlier while working as a producer, and being aware of the arrangements commissioned by Phil Spector, White chose to collaborate with the arranger Gene Page. Unable to read music, White would lay down a basic piano track with a chorus to give Page an impression of the overall idea behind the song and hum out the parts for the arrangement. Together, Page and White would then fashion the rhythm track and the strings, and finally White's voice would be added.[13] Recalling the process of composition of 'Never Gonna Give Ya Up' from his second solo LP, *Stone Gon'*, White tells a story involving him standing in front of the microphone in the studio with no prior preparation. 'There's no way in hell you can write those kinds of lyrics,' says White, 'you have to turn down the lights and close your eyes . . . and you just start rapping.'[14] Significantly, together White and Page developed a different feel for the strings. 'People were used to violins as a swaying, flowing sound, but I used them . . . as a rhythm instrument.'[15] Apparently at White's urging, Michael Jackson commissioned Quincy Jones to fully realize this rhythmic use of strings on a vocal track at the end of the decade on 'Don't Stop 'Til You Get Enough' (1979), updating the sound Jones developed with Charles in the late 1950s and Sinatra in the mid-1960s.

While Page was White's right arm when it came to the string orchestrations, since the attitude of the music couldn't be transcribed, White was always on hand in the studio to impress on the session players the desired feel.[16] New musical opportunities presented themselves as a result, White being able to identify 'a little space where I can slip in a beautiful little lick on the harpsichord or piano'.[17] With Ray Parker Jr coordinating them, White added five extra guitarists to Page's original orchestra. Initially Page felt this was a waste, as they were drowned out by the orchestra, but eventually the parts and counterparts blended incredibly well together.[18] Besides the lines written for the guitars, White hummed out licks for tenor solos, accents for horns and complex patterns between drummers and bassists.[19]

Laid down at Whitney Recording Studios in the Glendale district of LA, White's first solo LP, *I've Got So Much to Give*, is divided up between two contrasting moods, with Side 2 focusing on the upbeat aspects of romance. 'I'm Gonna Love You Just a Little More Baby', the final track on Side 2, begins with a type of groove that no one on the session had heard before. One attendee remembers how 'immediately the harpsichord came on, [and] Gene [Page] ran down the hall yelling, "Barry White's gonna be a star!" There were no grooves like this one before.'[20] At White's instruction, the harpsicord intersects with a drum pattern laid down by Ed Greene that attests to White's early experience on drums while working as a producer, on one occasion even accompanying Earl Nelson at the Apollo in Harlem in early 1966. Not surprisingly, this distinctive beat was sampled by numerous hip-hop artists, from the Notorious B.I.G. to Nas.

Veering away from his usual mode of bathos towards pathos, *I've Got So Much to Give* includes one of White's few torch ballads, 'Bring Back My Yesterday'. By portraying a character clinging on to the past, the track brings to a close Side 1 of the LP, devoted to the negative aspects of romance. Marking the slow tempo, the track opens with a cymbal being tapped by Greene, and then White, further pursuing the phone rap from the previous year, begins talking, as if reasoning with an estranged romantic interlocutor. A harpsichord plays the basic melody while an oboe picks it out in a higher register. White's pleading rap continues. Gradually more instruments coalesce around Jack Perry's harpsichord, followed by a brief instrumental break as the central theme is repeated. Singing in full emotive voice, White then re-enters with the word 'yesterday' and the arrangement takes off. Never has there been a voice in popular music so secure in the depth of its bass-baritone register; not even the deep-voiced singers of the past – including Billy Eckstine in the 1940s and Lou Rawls in the 1950s – luxuriated in their physicality to this degree. Following another verse, the first chorus finds the harpsichord riff played underneath the main refrain of the title, rhyming the words 'yesterday' and 'away'. When the couplet is repeated, White sings 'away' with such a raspy bottom note, it almost sounds as though he's missed it. Several listens prove this not to be the case: Frank Kejmar's engineering captures every vocal nuance. When asked during an interview if he considered himself to be a singer, White replied: 'No, Barry White is a carrier. He has a sound. But, no, he isn't a singer. Maybe he is a phraser! But he can take a melody and a message and deliver it. Instead of a voice, he has a way of delivering.'[21] For once, White is too modest.

Following *I've Got So Much to Give*, White further refined his sound with *Stone Gon'* (1973), *Can't Get Enough* (1974) and *Just Another Way to Say I Love You* (1975). Together these four LPs greatly impacted Gaye, and shaped the sinuous disco-funk of *I Want You* (1976). Biographer and confidant David Ritz recalls how Gaye spoke of the degree he 'loved White's brand of schmaltz and sugar-coated strings, viewing such arrangements as appropriate vehicles for expressing physical passion'.[22] Knowing Gaye was unsure of which direction to move in following *Let's Get It On* (1973), Motown founder Berry Gordy played him a new suite of songs jointly written by Leon Ware and Arthur 'T-Boy' Ross that were devoted precisely to physical passion. Conscious of the success of their song 'I Wanna Be Where You Are', written for Michael Jackson, Berry then played 'I Want You' for Gaye.[23] The next day Gaye was ready to do the Ware and Ross album. If the vocals on *I Want You* are distinctly Gaye, then the rhythmic role played by the strings in the arrangement is courtesy of White and Page.

Recently accentuated in Lord Finesse's 'I Want You (Underboss Remix)' (2020), the title track of Gaye's *I Want You* is anchored by a propulsive conga beat and rhythmic strings. In unison with the rhythm, during the track's intro, Gaye utters a series of guttural moans. As the beat becomes more insistent, a triple-tracked Gaye harmonizes with himself. Co-arranged by Ware, and with frequent White collaborator Parker Jr on guitar, the density of the orchestration is new to Gaye, with strings and rhythm section deftly interplaying. As with Page's arrangements for White, the strings serve a rhythmic function, accentuating the groove. What Ware had written as a sensual romantic ballad, Gaye transforms into a meditation on the possibility of unrequited eroticism. Gaye's self-harmonizing using multiple voices, each with its own distinct texture, is taken to new heights on *I Want You*. Pushing the idea to its furthest extreme – and racking up the studio hours – the new 24-track console allows Ware to suffuse Gaye's multi-tracked voice into the warp and weft of the instrumental tracks. 'Overdubbing those voices – stacking the vocals – was a technique he mastered,' recalls Jan Gaye, and 'each of these voices was unique – a sweet falsetto, a tender midrange, a sexual growl, a bottommost plea'.[24] Equipment pressed into the service of technique would be of little consequence were it not for the ability of Gaye's multi-tracked voice to envelop you in layer after layer of modulated timbral texture. To create the ambience required to sing so emotively, Gaye commissioned a purpose-built private recording studio in Hollywood on Sunset Boulevard in 1975, eulogized by Drake's song 'Marvins Room' (2011). For the most part, Gaye sang using a hand-held mic while relaxing on a couch next to the console in the control room.[25]

Precisely because of the proximity to White's sound, on its release, *I Want You* received Gaye's most negative reviews to date. 'With Barry White on the wane,' complained *Rolling Stone*, 'Marvin Gaye seems determined to take over as soul's master philosopher in the bedroom, a position that requires little but an affectation of constant, rather jaded horniness.'[26] Gaye's drive to express his sexuality undeniably became repetitive, but to claim that recording *I Want You* takes only a 'jaded horniness' is simply wrong-headed. *Down Beat* was just as harsh, describing the LP as 'slush for disco dancers' in the 'bogus over-blown manner of Barry White'.[27] The reviews failed to acknowledge the specific qualities held by either of their voices. By contrast, the criticism of Gaye would have been extremely appropriate to Sinatra's disco sides, with the pumped-up versions of 'All or Nothing at All' or 'Night and Day' orchestrated by Joe Beck being recorded a year later in 1977.

Barry White, c. 1980.

Couched in terms of the play between the sentimental and the sensual and the opportunities it provides for expressing gay sexuality, Richard Dyer's essay 'In Defence of Disco' (1979) provides apt reasoning for an account of White's and Gaye's vocal innovations. 'The lyrics of popular song', whether from the American song book or self-penned, writes Dyer, 'place its tunes firmly within a conceptualization of romance as emanating from "inside" the heart or the soul . . . thus the yearning cadences of popular song express an erotic yearning of the inner person, not the body.'[28] 'Disco refuses this,' Dyer continues: 'not only are the lyrics often more directly physical and the delivery more raunchy', but the music is 'insistently rhythmic in a way that popular song is not'.[29] The same is true of funk and disco funk. Announcing a shift towards a more rhythmic type of vocal music in the mid-1970s, White's *I've Got So Much to Give* and Gaye's *I Want You* both treat the voice as a further rhythmic instrument, rather than something to be overlayed onto a backing track.

In emphasizing its existence as an instrument, the crooner's voice on these LPS is particularly expressive of the body.

An overlooked coda to White's role in expanding the crooner archetype to encompass the producer took place in 1984, as White details:

> Marvin got in touch with [*Soul Train* producer] Don Cornelius to try to find me. I had just come back from a tour . . . and as I was going through the Los Angeles airport, everyone was coming up and telling me how great this new album was going to be. 'What new album?' I asked. 'The one with you and Marvin.' It wasn't until I got home that I saw in *Billboard* Marvin had announced I was going to produce his next album. The next thing I knew the phone is ringing. Don Cornelius . . . 'Chiefie,' he said, which was what we called each other, 'how you doin?' We talked for a few seconds, and then he said, 'B.W., somebody here wants to talk to you.' The next thing I knew, Marvin was on the phone. 'B.W., . . . you got to produce my next album.'[30]

Considering the barrage of critique *I Want You* received due to its perceived proximity to White, and the hit Gaye enjoyed with the largely self-composed, arranged and produced *Midnight Love* (1982), it's nothing less than intriguing that Gaye chose him to produce the follow-up LP in 1984. Neither of White's recent LPS, *Change* (1982) and *Dedicated* (1983), developed the crooner archetype to a noticeable degree by embracing new technologies as effectively as *Midnight Love*, which was largely written and for the first time largely performed by Gaye.[31] So why go to White? New provocatively titled songs typified by 'Sanctified Pussy' and 'Let Me Spank Your Booty (My Masochistic Beauty)' suggest Gaye immersing himself even more deeply in the subject-matter explored eight years before on *I Want You*.[32] Just imagine the groove from White's 'I'm Gonna Love

You Just a Little More Baby' put together with Gaye's lyrical ideas for 'Sanctified Pussy'![33] Together, White and Gaye may have produced the first mature hip-hop LP, including, of course, the overbearing chauvinism and problematic aggressive imagery associated with the genre.[34]

White took the phone call from Gaye on the Friday and the two planned to meet the following Monday. But on Sunday, 1 April 1984, White received a call to say Gaye had been murdered. As neither of Gaye's demos for the two new songs, or the backing tracks White had immediately begun to assemble after receiving Gaye's call, have ever been made available, there is no way of knowing which direction the two would have taken things, or whether the crooner model expanded by White could have yielded engaging results in the service of Gaye's music. As it was, it took over four more years before anything coming near to what White and Gaye may have achieved together based on their past releases was realized and for West Coast rap to become a fully fledged art form. With it, the vocalist as producer and label owner, as part of an African American artists' pursuit of self-determination and institution-building, became an acknowledged way of operating. White's expansion of the role of the crooner as vocalist and songwriter to encompass the producer is a significant part of the history of the archetype.

4

David Bowie: 'Word on a Wing' (1976)

T he scene is Cherokee Studios, Los Angeles, in 1975, and David Bowie is about to meet Frank Sinatra. According to Cherokee's manager:

One night Sinatra said, 'You've got this Bowie guy in here. How is he?'. . . Then Bowie would say, 'Oh my God, Sinatra's here. I'd love to meet him'. So we set up a dinner with the two of them . . . They came back to the studio in Sinatra's limo and at that point it was pretty obvious that they were becoming fast friends . . . They visited each other's sessions. He heard some of the *Station to Station* playbacks, and he liked Bowie's version of the . . . song 'Wild is the Wind'. David even sang a harmony part on one of Sinatra's songs.[1]

Bowie's desire to meet Sinatra speaks volumes about his perception of himself as a crooner at this point. So does Bowie's very styling of himself as the character of the Thin White Duke in 1976: the crisp, white blouson shirt overlaid by a tailored black waistcoat, and the pleated trousers with knife-sharp creases are arguably the first iteration of what can be termed the 'meta-crooner': a crooner who knowingly adopts the visual and sonic cues associated with the archetype of the crooner. This would have been made all the more apparent to Bowie upon meeting Sinatra, then dressed in typical

London, 1974: an RCA Records publicity still showing rock-and-roll musician David Bowie working in the studio during the recording of his *Diamond Dogs* album, which was recorded between October 1973 and February 1974 in London and the Netherlands.

conservative 1970s menswear, all broad collars and loudly patterned shirts and jackets. With a few subtle adjustments, it was as if the Bowie of 1975 were a pastiche of the Sinatra of 1945.

The Thin White Duke gains part of its distinctiveness because it comes straight after the desiccated white soul boy of *Young Americans*, itself replacing the androgynous Aladdin Sane and Ziggy Stardust. The technicolour cartoon-like eccentricity and flamboyance of Bowie's earlier characters, too often taking the focus away from his voice, are replaced with the Thin White Duke's icy monochrome veneer. Beneath this veneer, Bowie continues to pursue the androgyny of the earlier characters in a different way. The claimed bisexuality Bowie announced during an infamous interview in 1972 – theatricalized with Ziggy Stardust – was still being pursued in 1975, but with a greater degree of subtlety. In 'Notes on Camp' (1964), Susan Sontag defines 'the androgyne [as] certainly one of the great images of Camp sensibility'. It draws 'on a mostly unacknowledged truth of taste: the most refined form of sexual attractiveness . . . consists in going against the grain of one's sex'.[2] To this profile of camp taste Bowie injects a more abrasive political and psychological profile, describing the Thin White Duke as a 'very Aryan, fascist type; a would-be romantic with absolutely no emotion at all but who spouted a lot of neo-romance'.[3] Beneath the Thin White Duke's surface lies a cocaine-riddled person full of self-doubt, who, in lyrics and interviews, desperately reaches for random points of orientation, including religion, national socialism and the occult. But the relative coolness of the character affords Bowie the opportunity to turn out some of the most intense crooning of the decade.

Station to Station contrasts two poached musical elements: the mechanical angularity of Krautrock – the repetitive mechanical beats of Kraftwerk and the buzzsaw guitar of Can – and Philly soul's rhythmic funk set on a bed of strings. Of his approach to making *Young Americans*, Bowie later commented on how he juxtaposed 'very un-soully lyrics over very soul-influenced music'.[4] The comment Bowie makes in concluding this point in the interview is key. 'It's always taking something,' he says, 'and just twisting it.'[5] Bowie's ability to juxtapose antithetical elements – whether it be soul music and 'un-soully' lyrics with *Young Americans* or Krautrock and Philly soul on *Station to Station* – by 'twisting' them together is indeed fundamental to the success of *Station to Station*. Bowie's crooning as the Thin White Duke adds a further twist.

Across *Station to Station*'s six songs, Bowie seemingly allows the listener to hear the Thin White Duke think out loud. Lyrics referring to the European canon from the album's eponymous opening track not only announce Bowie's intention to leave America and return to Europe, in the form of Berlin, but revisit Europe's musical canon, turning away from Philly soul towards both the text of German Singspiel and the instrumentation of Krautrock. Providing further ballast for this reading, in an interview, Bowie recalls owning 'an import of [Kraftwerk's] *Autobahn* in the States, probably in the year it came out, 1974', that is, when *Young Americans* was being cut: 'I came across Tangerine Dream and Can and eventually Neu! and this whole new sound happening in Germany.'[6] While making one album, Bowie was continually feeding in influences to inform the next one.

Following the move to LA in March 1975, Bowie remained in New Mexico from June through to August to play the disaffected alien Thomas Jerome Newton in Nicolas Roeg's *The Man Who Fell to Earth*. Roeg rejected the tracks that Bowie recorded for the film score, but the film itself afforded Bowie the opportunity to fashion the Thin White Duke character. 'Nic exerts such as tremendous influence over one psychologically', explains Bowie, 'that one does carry the weight of the image around for a bit afterwards.'[7] For the Thin White Duke's costume worn during the *Station to Station* tour, Bowie, working with designer Ola Hudson, pulled the clothes out of Newton's character. On returning to LA, Bowie eventually moved to Stone Canyon Road in the woods above Bel-Air, and shifted attention to his next album.

The BBC documentary *David Bowie: Cracked Actor* (1975) catches Bowie sitting in the back of a limousine as it traverses LA. An ema-ciated Bowie remarks on empathizing with a fly floating in a carton of milk he is drinking from. 'There's a foreign body in it, you see? And it's getting a lot of milk,' Bowie points out to the interviewer. 'That's kind of how I felt. A foreign body,' Bowie says of LA: 'I couldn't help but soak it up. I hated it when I first came here, I couldn't see any of it.'[8] Expanding, Bowie remarks on how the city filled a vast expanse of his imagination, becoming what he refers to as a 'mythic land'. The documentary then cuts to a view of the interior of a guided-tour bus making its way through the 'mythic land' of the Bel-Air area of the city, past the home of Dean Martin and the former home of, according to the guide, his 'best buddy' Frank Sinatra.

David Bowie live during *Thin White Duke* tour, Rotterdam Ahoy, Netherlands, 13 May 1976.

The first musician Bowie recruited to play on *Station to Station* was guitarist Carlos Alomar, and, together with drummer Dennis Davis and bass player George Murray, they laid down the rhythm tracks at Cherokee Studios. 'With the rhythm section locked down, you had a bird's-eye view of the whole [thing],' says Alomar.[9] 'We were able to get the skeleton of what we needed, which allowed the other musicians to have a bigger palette of sounds to work with.'[10] Further instrumentalists were added at that point, principally lead guitarist Earl Slick and keyboard player Roy Bittan. Alomar adds, 'The different ways we were looking at arrangements allowed

David Bowie arriving at the Cherokee Recording Studio in Hollywood, California, 1976.

David to look at the music the way he looks at words, which is to cut them up.'[11] Finally, Bowie would do his vocals, with Warren Peace's backing voice subtly accentuating them in places.

The first track from *Station to Station* to be recorded was 'Golden Years'. Sequenced as the second song on Side 1, this sounds out of place on the LP and would surely have been better left as a stand-alone single, as originally released in November 1975, providing a neat parenthesis between *Young Americans* (March 1975) and *Station to Station* (January 1976). As it is, 'Golden Years' finds Bowie demonstrating lessons learnt from Luther Vandross during *Young Americans* regarding vocal arrangements – albeit in this case by multi-tracking himself – especially as the song concludes with the cascading refrain about running for shadows. Working together with Bowie in the studio afforded producer Harry Maslin an extreme close-up of his process. 'He was famous for going into the corner . . . and writing some lyrics, which is what he did on "Golden Years",' says Maslin, as Bowie 'literally went to the bathroom and came back with the lyric, went to the mike, and did the song in one take'.[12] The first album track to be recorded that heralded a breakthrough to a new sound was 'Stay', which Alomar judiciously characterized as having 'that more glass-breaking rock and roll-ness to it. We didn't want to just go back to making another funk-R&B record.'[13] While the rhythm 'n' blues funk of *Young Americans* is still present in 'Stay', it's now polished to a brilliant sheen; and the razor-sharp guitar riffs that exited after *Diamond Dogs* (1974) make a dramatic return, as Slick's gnarly lead guitar lines wind in and out of the rhythmic patterns Alomar lays down.

The final track on Side 2, 'Wild Is the Wind', is the one most thought of as spotlighting Bowie's crooning abilities. With only a relatively basic rhythmic track to accompany it and Slick on acoustic instead of the usual electric guitar, Bowie's vocals are pushed to the front, recalling the nakedly emotional version of the song from a decade earlier by Nina Simone, whom Bowie befriended the previous year in Paris. *Rolling Stone* critic Cameron Crowe's observations of the track's vocal session lucidly set the scene:

It's a late fall evening, 1975. A single yellow light shines overhead. Hands in pockets, Bowie asks to hear the still-unfinished track he's been working on. 'Wild Is the Wind' fills the room with sound. It's lush, and stark, and the track is nearing completion. He lifts an acoustic guitar and strums out a rhythm part, kneeling now, directly under that yellow light. The effect is strikingly cinematic, a marriage of sight and sound. Many a control room would be buzzing with meaningless chatter, technical conversation, or just plain small-talk. Not here. It's silent here. Producer Harry Maslin watches quietly, riveted. Another cornerstone of the album is almost in place. 'A good day for ideas,' says Bowie. His hat cocked over his carrot-coloured hair, a blonde streak at the centre, for a moment he looks like young Frank Sinatra dipped in red-and-yellow ink.[14]

As the album's closing track, it's logical that 'Wild is the Wind' mark its highpoint and summation. Logical, perhaps, but not the case. The final track on Side 1, 'Word on a Wing', is actually the one in which Bowie's voice reaches new heights. Starting with Bittan's simple piano figure, underpinned by a warm synth bed, the rhythm section soon kicks in for a few bars, the loping beat providing Slick's subtle lead guitar the space to weave around Bittan's repeated keyboard figure. Enter Bowie's voice – with a line about someone walking out of his dreams and into his life – which feels deeper and mellower than on previous albums, more mature sounding. Until this point, the vocal is much less affected than usual; there are no invasive effects or double tracking to mask it. The voice as instrument perfectly complements the voice as person, with a more subtle character role than those adopted earlier in the decade to parley between the two. A further line and then the opening refrain is repeated but with a little bit of lift. Now the first surprise: a change in vocal tone with the line referring to being 'born again'. Underpinned by a backing voice, presumably Peace's, here Bowie's voice rises into the tenor range. At the same time as the 'born again' line is repeated, Bittan's piano begins to swirl over the top of the rhythm, followed by another change in vocal approach. Now Bowie sounds almost conversational when he delivers a line, emphasizing that just because he's a believer in religion, it doesn't cancel out his ability to think independently. This tactic of pulling a phrase or stanza out of a song by using a different, more conversational tone to comment on it comes, in contrast to Barry White's developed earlier in the decade, directly from the stage and particularly Anthony Newley, a key vocalist and performer for Bowie. Bowie deploys Newley's vocal device in a more subtle and less stagey way here, so that it serves as a corrective to the plea made in the song's previous line. '[Newley] used to make his points with this broad Cockney accent,' Bowie remarked, 'and I decided that I'd use that now and again to drive a point home.'[15] Following a second Newley-esque line sung in conversational tone, Bowie really throws his voice for the first time in the song, with a line imploring to the 'Lord', the singer offering his 'Word on a Wing'. The word 'Lord' is particularly emphasized, sounding like throttled histrionics. A further line and the 'Lord' is again called on, this time in falsetto. Rather than using falsetto like Marvin Gaye, to emphasize the sensual undercurrent of a lyric, Bowie uses it to convey a sense of the protagonist's repeating of a refrain as if out loud to himself while mulling it over, instead of to an audience, as with the earlier Newley-influenced passage.

But 'Word on a Wing' is only halfway through at this point. The best is still to come, as the 'Lord' phrase of the chorus is repeated. The second time the refrain about the strange land is sung, it sounds singularly amazing. The words at the start of the phrase are seemingly held in the throat and contrast sharply with the phrase about a strange land, which is dealt with in a deeper voice that sits more in the chest. The effect is dramatic. 'At first I thought [those songs] didn't seem to fit,' says Alomar, 'but they took the album into a more human area. They were a release moment so that he could actually cry – there was pain there, and he was able to open up on those songs.'[16] Bowie refers to becoming 'over-emotive' at this point and going 'through great waves of despondency and ecstasy' after having 'kept a lot of things pretty well repressed for a few years'.[17] It's as if the icy facade of the Thin White Duke throws any emotional phrase forward because of the contrast. Very few singers are able to underpin a high sense of technical virtuosity with such a degree of emotional depth in a way that is laced with the nihilistic conceptual acuity of Bowie as the Thin White Duke. 'Word on a Wing' is nothing less than one of the decade's most inventive torch songs, sung by one of the most powerful crooners.

While initially it seems that the song is about a lost love – man or woman – Bowie claimed the lyrics were addressing God. 'There's a song – "Word on a Wing" – . . . on the new album that I wrote . . . as a hymn. What better way can a man give thanks for achieving something that he had dreamed of achieving, than doing it with a hymn?'[18] This contrasts with Bowie's later comment on the album: 'The "Station to Station" track itself is very much concerned with the stations of the cross [and all] the references within the piece are to do with the Kabbala . . . It's the nearest album to a magick treatise that I've written. It's an extremely dark album.'[19] Dark it may be, but 'Word on a Wing' is nevertheless a powerfully realized torch song.

Bowie's use of the voice as instrument is perfectly aligned with the voice as body, person and character in 'Word on a Wing'. No other singer is able to do this to the same degree in this period. Of his voice at this time, Bowie commented that

> it's only now that I've got the necessary confidence to sing like that . . . When I started rehearsing with the band for this [*Station to Station*] tour, I suddenly realized I was enjoying singing again. I hadn't enjoyed it in a long time. It was just a way to get my songs across. But when I started rehearsing, I began enjoying it and I found I actually had a voice . . . My voice has improved in leaps and bounds . . . I'd really like to be recognised as a singer . . . Maybe I just want to be a crooner.[20]

This neatly corresponds with Bowie's interest in Sinatra and the drive behind their meeting, and speaks volumes about what was being aimed for at the time and the lineage Bowie wanted to contribute to. While duetting with Bing Crosby in 1977, Bowie was nearer to Sinatra in terms of vocal authority. As Crowe judiciously observed,

British rock singer and actor David Bowie performs with American pop singer Bing Crosby for the TV special *Bing Crosby's Merrie Olde Christmas*, London, England, December 1977.

81

the *Station to Station*-era Bowie was 'Frank Sinatra dipped in red-and-yellow ink'. Of all Sinatra's songs, while 'That's What God Looks Like to Me from *Trilogy* (1980) is the closest to 'Word on a Wing' in subject-matter, the rapturous 'Ebb Tide' from *Only the Lonely* (1958) recalls Bowie's track in the way emotional intensity is built up throughout the duration of a song. Turning from the darkness of the rest of the *Only the Lonely* LP, 'Ebb Tide' is not strictly a torch ballad; it is more of a romantic one. As Bowie vocally reaches a crescendo on 'Word on a Wing' with the lyrics about a 'strange land', on 'Ebb Tide' Sinatra peaks with the lines about being able to feel. Listening to the songs side by side, it's impossible to say which crooner is the most affecting. Both harness their technical vocal authority to emotive ends.

Bowie contributes not only a dynamic undercurrent of sexual ambiguity to the lineage of the crooner, absent until this point, but a power and inventiveness that marked popular understandings of the voice as instrument. Crucially, Bowie explodes the previous ways that the voice as instrument had been expressive of a body by blurring the relationship between the performer (David Bowie) and the character being inhabited (the Thin White Duke) in each song. This goes some way to explain why the Bowie of 1976 serves as a crucial hinge in time within the history of the crooner. In harnessing the technical ability of Sinatra and Walker and using it within a contemporary setting that channels rock and funk, Bowie fashions a distinctive approach, producing a series of incredible vocal performances but also anticipating the new-wave crooners to come.

5

Bryan Ferry: 'When She Walks (in the Room)' (1978)

Bryan Ferry arrived in Los Angeles six months after David Bowie left for Berlin, to develop material for his LP *The Bride Stripped Bare* (1978). A few years earlier, amid the cultural fervour of the late 1960s, the historical crooner model appropriated by Ferry and Bowie may not have been deemed so attractive – accounting for the difficulties Scott Walker encountered at the time. However, by the early 1970s this was beginning to change. '[Sinatra] has an immaculateness which I admire,' Ferry commented, after selecting *Songs for Swinging Lovers* (1956) as one of his favourite LPs. 'I love that mohair suit in the spotlight business.'[1] Typified by his first solo LP, *These Foolish Things* (1973), titled after a Cole Porter song covered by Sinatra in 1962, the rest of Ferry's solo career would be driven by a contemporary reworking of the crooner archetype. *The Bride Stripped Bare* is key to this.

Crucial to Ferry's reworking of the crooner archetype is the use of songs as readymades. Following Ferry's mentor, Richard Hamilton, and his fascination with Marcel Duchamp, *These Foolish Things* announces the strategy to render the songs of the past as so many readymades, available to be re-recorded. '[When] I took a song that was by somebody else, and did my own version of it,' explains Ferry, 'I was adding my stamp to it . . . Like a readymade – a song as a readymade.'[2] Using the monotone voice associated with Fred Astaire, 'These Foolish Things' finds Ferry highlighting its condition as a

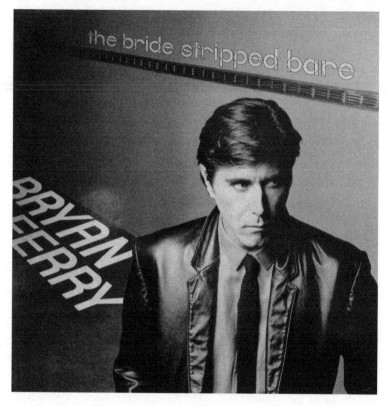

Bryan Ferry, *The Bride Stripped Bare* (1978), vintage vinyl album cover.

readymade by singing the song as if playing a character in a film from the time of its writing. Conceptually acute Ferry's strategy may have been, but *These Foolish Things* is emotionally vapid in terms of the weight of the interpretations of the songs it covers. 'Smoke Gets in Your Eyes' from Ferry's second solo LP, *Another Time, Another Place* (1974), is slightly more engaging: it maintains Ferry's concept of lifting a song from the past and placing it in the present but extends it by adding a more emotive dimension to its performance. The ongoing use of the readymade in both song and image allows Ferry to smuggle the historic crooner in through the back door of 1970s rock music. While Ferry opted for a dark crew-necked T-shirt for the cover of *These Foolish Things* to provide a contrast with Roxy

84

Music's elaborate glam costumes of the same year, TV appearances from 1973 in which the title track is performed see Ferry dressed in a white tuxedo, a look extended to the cover of *Another Time, Another Place*. Where Bowie fashions a new persona – in the form of the Thin White Duke – that incorporates aspects of the past but totally reshapes them, Ferry treats the image of the historic crooner as he treats songs: a readymade to be picked up and reused. From the broad-lapelled, Antony Price-designed jacket down to the wafer-thin gold watch, on the cover of *Another Time, Another Place* Ferry looks exactly like a crooner from the 1930s, albeit recontextualized within the 1970s fascination with the era popularized by the 1974 film adaptation of *The Great Gatsby* directed by Jack Clayton. Where Bowie forcefully plays up his characters by fleshing out their personalities, Ferry's characters – from the sci-fi leopard-skin androgyny of the first Roxy Music album to the Rick Blaine tuxedo-wearing character, and on to the American GI of *Siren* (1975) – are both less androgynous and more lightly worn. Nowhere are Ferry's personas fleshed out as characters, either lyrically or in terms of specific vocal attributes.

Before turning to the blues in the late 1970s, Ferry fully embraces camp in the cover versions that constitute the bulk of his early solo albums. 'The way of Camp', Sontag wrote in 1964 – while Ferry was still studying with Hamilton – is 'in terms of the degree of artifice, of stylization'.[3] Referring to *These Foolish Things* in an interview, Ferry describes working with existing material, declaring himself 'a song stylist'.[4] Since to emphasize style is to slight content, for Sontag, 'it goes without saying that the Camp sensibility is disengaged.'[5] By increasing the pace and adding backing singers and sound effects, Ferry neutralizes and disengages the political content of Bob Dylan's 'A Hard Rain's a-Gonna Fall', the opener of *These Foolish Things*. 'Camp is a vision of the world in terms of style – but a particular kind of style.' 'It is', Sontag specifies, 'the love of the exaggerated, the "off".'[6] Ferry's version of 'A Hard Rain's a-Gonna

Fall' finds a love of the exaggerated, the 'off', at its most extreme. Besides camping up versions of songs like Dylan's, Ferry is also drawn to songs from the 1930s with an existing level of camp already associated with them. The leap from Fred Astaire's 'These Foolish Things' (1935) to Ferry's version is much shorter than the one from Dylan's 'A Hard Rain's a-Gonna Fall'. An aspect of Ferry's approach to camp also derives from notions of aristocratic taste. 'Aristocracy is a position vis-à-vis culture,' writes Sontag, 'and the history of Camp taste is part of the history of snob taste.'[7] With a few exceptions, whenever Ferry is photographed or filmed at this point, it is within an aristocratic setting, whether it be the luxurious splendour of his Holland Park apartment or a Bel-Air house with a swimming pool amid the Jet-Set. After pointing out that 'no authentic aristocrats in the old sense still exist to sponsor special tastes,' Sontag concludes that the bearer of this taste is 'an improvised self-elected class, mainly homosexuals, who constitute themselves as aristocrats of taste'.[8] Alongside the aristocratic pose, Ferry's adoption of the pose of a crooner explores the undercurrents of camp, if not in terms of its actual sexual drives. Even though Ferry's approach to camp does not express an actual ambiguity in terms of sexual preference as Bowie's does, by piloting what can be termed the 'camp crooner', Ferry does interrogate rock's dominant version of masculinity, a process of questioning that slows down by the mid-1970s and is then reversed in the latter part of the decade as Ferry comes to embody it.

Unlike Bowie, who only occasionally turns to the torch ballad, Ferry perpetually reworks the genre in the guise of the crooner. Until *The Bride Stripped Bare*, each of Ferry's attempts at a torch song was written using a narrative device that places the narrator at one remove from the subject, reflected in the non-emotional vocal approach. 'I always wrote as a character,' says Ferry, '[and] in some songs it rings more true to me, then there are others that are obviously me assuming a role.'[9] This process starts with one of the

Bryan Ferry and Roxy Music singing 'A Hard Rain's a-Gonna Fall' in the studio, June 1973 during Ferry's recording of his first solo album, *These Foolish Things*.

most unusual torch ballads ever written, 'In Every Dream Home a Heartache' from *For Your Pleasure*, in the form of an ode to a mail-order blow-up doll. No other lyricist in 1973 could produce such a warped torch ballad.

A year later, in 1974, comes 'Bitter Sweet' from Roxy Music's *Country Life*, the lyrics reading like the private reflections of a night-club singer, accentuated by the Weimar-era bar-room vamp of the chorus. Much of the band's following album, *Siren* (1975), deals with the theme of unrequited love, albeit at one remove, especially on the set's final track, 'Just Another High'. While Roxy Music fell silent at this point until 1979, Ferry collected all of his recent solo singles together on the LP *Let's Stick Together* (1976), the only torch ballad being a version of John Lennon's 'It's Only Love'. Released the same year as Bowie's highpoint, *Station to Station*, the LP represents something of a low for Ferry. *In Your Mind* from a year later fares better, and is Ferry's first solo LP to consist entirely of self-penned songs but contains no torch ballads – a situation that was soon to change.

'A very, very emotional album', is how Ferry refers to *The Bride Stripped Bare*, its title proudly sporting another Duchamp reference, this time to his *The Bride Stripped Bare by Her Bachelors, Even* (1915–23).[10] Reconstructed by Hamilton in 1965–6 while Ferry was one of his students in Newcastle, Duchamp's *The Bride Stripped Bare by Her Bachelors, Even* is often explained as presenting the impossibility of resolution between men and women, hence Ferry's choice of it for the title of an LP including torch ballads. Co-produced by a team that included producer Steve Nye, *The Bride Stripped Bare* was, like Bowie's *Station to Station*, mostly written in LA, the atmosphere in the city making Ferry feel 'even more introspective than . . . before'.[11] Ferry refers to track two on Side 1 of the album, 'Can't Let Go', as his 'meisterwerk about LA. It's an album about Los Angeles condensed into one song [as] I did often feel violent there, because it's so placid.'[12] Focusing on the area of LA where wealthy actors and directors lived, one of the many cutting lines in 'Can't Let Go' refers to Bel-Air as a graveyard. In the 1970s, it seems like the city greatly impacted any European crooner operating there.

Alongside writing this material in LA, Ferry began to assemble a new band to work with on the forthcoming LP. Some of the members were already associated with the city's contemporary music scene. The idea of Waddy Wachtel, who Ferry was introduced to at a Jackson Browne recording session in LA, 'playing with Neil Hubbard

... was very exciting', remarks Ferry, accounting for the blues-bent character of *The Bride Stripped Bare*.[13] But where Bowie recorded his album in LA during an extended stay before leaving for a three-year sojourn in Berlin, Ferry spent only six months in LA to write – July to December 1977 – and then left to record his album in Montreux. Following the break-up with the cover star of *Siren*, Jerry Hall, by Ferry's own account the production of *The Bride Stripped Bare* was an intense and emotional experience, enhanced by the desolate atmosphere of an out-of-season resort:

> The only thing to do there was to make music. There were no distractions. It turned out to be the strangest album I've ever done. There was such a crazed atmosphere in Montreux. There was this band of musicians just stuck there . . . We just moved out there and dug in. I'm really searching for the words to describe it. It was possibly the most soulful musical experience I've ever been through. It was very remote and very lonely and very crazed.[14]

Ferry describes wanting *The Bride Stripped Bare* to be 'extracts . . . of various styles and moods', hence what he refers to as the 'art-conceit of the title', as Duchamp's work 'was full of strange elements adding up to one thing, one statement'.[15] These extracts included shifts in mood from the fast-paced 'Sign of the Times', slowing down with mid-paced numbers like J. J. Cale's 'Same Old Blues' and 'This Island Earth', and further still with the ballads 'Carrickfergus' and 'When She Walks in the Room'. In terms of the writing method underpinning the self-penned songs, Ferry's publicist Rex Balfour comments on how Ferry

> would arrive at the studio after being up most of the night perfecting the lyrics, and would add them in one or two takes. Until that moment, nobody had any idea of what the song they

had been working on was about, or even what the melody line might be. But it worked: magically, each track was transformed from a complex instrumental sequence into a brilliantly-conceived whole.[16]

Positioned as *The Bride Stripped Bare*'s last track on Side 1, 'When She Walks in the Room' is the most effective torch ballad of Ferry's

Bryan Ferry with Jerry Hall, c. 1976.

career to date. Opening with a parlour-like motif from a string quartet, as if announcing the narrative action about to begin, the song proper starts after a brief drum fill. Against the slow tempo marked by the rhythm section of Herbie Flowers on upright bass, Rick Marotta on drums and Hubbard on guitar, Ferry begins to sketch a late-night party scene, interrupted by the entrance of a lost love walking into a room. Until this point, Ferry's voice is more resolute than plaintive. But this changes with the line about the laughter of the woman being referred to. The word 'laughter' is rendered using a trill, a form of vocal ornamentation constituted by a rapid alternation between two adjacent notes, so that it becomes 'lau-ghter'. The way the trill interrupts the pronunciation of the word injects a shake that conveys a sense of emotion. Overused, this technique becomes just another vocal quirk, but if used discerningly it can inject a sense of drama into a song's narrative. The scene having been set by the first verse, the string quartet's riff is repeated, this time underpinned by the rhythm section, to be followed by the next verse, which finds the narrator reflecting on his predicament. As the verses continue, the music slowly builds in rhythm and detail as the tempo subtly increases and the guitar occupies the remaining space which trebly blues fills. The final verse ends with a line about exiting the room through a door. As the music continues to swell, Ferry repeats this phrase. An instrumental interlude finds the rhythm and pace brought right back down again. Just the bass and drum continue for several bars with the occasional piano or guitar fill. The backing refrain using the title 'When She Walks (in the Room)', sung by Ferry and Wachtel together, then rides out the remaining 90 seconds of the track, each repetition being counterpointed by a different drum, piano or bass fill, until it fades. To fashion a more emotive form of crooning, Ferry seems to need to keep his tendency towards campness in check.

Ferry's voice develops very gradually in texture and quality up until *The Bride Stripped Bare*. Especially with Roxy Music, but also as a solo artist, there is a sense that Ferry uses his voice as another instrument, floating it somewhere within the mix. By contrast, as Bowie moves between characters, his voice not only changes but is rendered with much crisper contours in each mix, lending the impression of his voice being floated over the top of the instrumentation. Underpinning this could be Ferry's sense of just how comparatively insecure an instrument his voice is. This would account for why, on early LPS, Ferry's voice is often double-tracked, leading to a sort of phasing effect that blurs its precise contours. A common practice in the period – even a singer such as Lennon, with an incredibly rich tone, made use of it – in many cases, this form of double tracking only served to mask rather than accentuate interesting vocal characteristics. By the time of *In Your Mind* (1977), Ferry used double tracking less, and with *The Bride Stripped Bare* a year later, thankfully, not at all. The result is a type of vocal performance that, by permitting moments of fragility – allowing the voice to shake or strain – is also more emotive, and speaks to a more confident crooner. As with Walker and Bowie, Sinatra is also a point of reference for Ferry. When asked how his singing voice came to be, Ferry refers to Sinatra, Billie Holiday and Otis Redding in his answer: 'By accident. You hear things through the sensibility of all the people you ever liked who sang – all the R&B singers you appreciated and the jazz singers before that. And then you just sing without thinking.'[17] Even Ferry's vocal style is premised on the notion of the readymade.

Ferry's 'When She Walks in the Room' most recalls an overlooked Sinatra B-side from 1969: 'Forget to Remember'. Written by Teddy Randazzo and Victoria Pike and arranged by Don Costa, who worked with Sinatra on *A Man Alone* (1969), 'Forget to Remember' is also centred on a specific memory triggered by a room, with the narrator finding themselves alone at home, attempting to ignore items that belong to a now-absent partner. Rather than the event happening live in the space, as it does in Ferry's 'When She Walks in the Room', Sinatra's song is instead structured in terms of a memory triggered by objects belonging to the absent partner. Where Ferry's song gently builds as the chorus using the title refrain is repeated ad infinitum during the song's final segment, Sinatra's builds in tension until the final release in full voice with the single sequence of lines playing on the title 'Forget to Remember'. Close to the former in terms of its lyrical conceit, 'When She Walks in the Room' is by far Ferry's optimum moment as a crooner.

Following the first two Roxy Music albums and Brian Eno's exit, Ferry was by far less adventurous than Bowie, as indicated by Eno collaborating with the latter on the Berlin trilogy of LPS from 1977 to 1979. But Ferry was easily the more consistent of the two. In the 1970s, his writing and singing developed gradually from LP to LP, whereas Bowie was far more erratic, leaping from style to style. What Ferry lacked in terms of breadth was made up for in the depth with which each stylistic terrain is slowly explored. Ferry moved away from the voice as character and arrived at the voice as instrument and person in 1978 on the emotive *The Bride Stripped Bare*. By contrast, Bowie didn't arrive at this point until much later, if at all, remaining caught in the realm of the voice as character. Bowie's flashes of brilliance in terms of the torch ballad, characterized by tracks like 'Word on a Wing', contrast sharply with Ferry's consistent reworking of the genre, and with it, the crooner archetype, throughout the decade of the 1970s and beyond.

Poster for *One from the Heart* (dir. Francis Ford Coppola, 1982).

6

Tom Waits: 'Ruby's Arms' (1980)

In Los Angeles, June 1980, Tom Waits refined his distinctive gravel-laden approach to crooning by moving between two very different styles of music: that which featured on *Heartattack and Vine* (1980), recorded at the RCA Building in Hollywood, and that of the soundtrack to Francis Ford Coppola's *One from the Heart* (1982), recorded at Wally Heider's Studio 3, also in Hollywood. At the time, Waits knew the soundtrack for Coppola would interrupt his plans. 'By the time Francis asked me to write those songs,' Waits reveals, 'I had really decided I was going to move away from that whole lounge thing. [Coppola] said he wants a "lounge operetta," and I was thinking, "Well, you're about a couple of years too late."'[1]

In order to force the transition that his music was on the cusp of, Waits had already changed his backdrop by relocating from Los Angeles to New York and taken a meeting with Jack Nitzsche, the producer who helped Neil Young move from the lush romanticism of *Harvest* (1972) to the edgier sonics of *Tonight's the Night* (1975). 'Yeah, I had some plans to explore new producers. I'd moved to New York for about five/six months, wanting to challenge myself with an entirely new environment,' admits Waits.[2] Besides meeting with Nitzsche, Waits also engaged in an initial discussion with Coppola in April, when Coppola visited New York to conduct auditions for *One from the Heart*. Coppola's pitch outlined how certain scenes would be built around Waits's songs, meaning that they would play

95

a much larger role than just providing background or atmosphere. The film would be like a very carefully designed Valentine, Coppola explained to Waits, and 'the singers would be like Hera and Zeus, commenting on this small community' of characters.[3] Enthralled by the idea of his songs being given such weight in the conception of a major film, the new type of crooning Waits was poised to embrace was put on hold, and the singer signed on to do the project. The idea of being to Coppola what Frank Sinatra and Nelson Riddle had been to Fred Kohlmar on the soundtrack to the musical *Pal Joey* (1957) was too enticing to turn down.

While working on the soundtrack necessitated a delay in the complete transformation of the crooner, it provided the impetus to push the very idiom of the cocktail-lounge troubadour that Waits had been operating in throughout the 1970s to the limit. Waits refers to how the slow production of *One from the Heart* over eighteen months triggered the intense writing and recording of *Heartattack and Vine* in a few weeks during a break in the film's schedule. Where the up-tempo tracks on *Heartattack and Vine* find Waits pushing forward towards the harder-edged sound of LPs such as *Swordfishtrombones* (1983), the *One from the Heart* soundtrack pulls him back in chronology to *Foreign Affairs* (1977) or even *Small Change* (1976). Often thought of as merely a transitional zone between two key periods, 1980 to 1981 was, in fact, a crucial eighteen months for Waits's refinement of a certain model of crooning.

Returning to LA in late April/early May of 1980 after meeting Coppola, Waits installed himself and his piano in wood-panelled offices with a 'David Niven feel' on the Zoetrope lot, the old Hollywood General studios on Las Palmas Avenue.[4] Brimming with Styrofoam cups, magazines, scraps of paper and whisky bottles, the office was a veritable thesaurus of visual detritus. The office came with a proximity to an industrious creative team. Waits temporarily revelled in joining a tradition of songwriters that went back decades:

I'd always admired the Tin Pan Alley writers, guys writing in brick buildings and hearing stuff like, 'Well, we need an opening song now, because we'll be opening in Poughkeepsie in two weeks. Come on, write something, then we'll run it up the flagpole and see if anybody salutes.' That kind of writing routine always looked attractive to me.[5]

The attraction would wear off, but not before it generated the necessary material. Once installed in this new place of work, Waits began composing. 'Sometimes to start the wheel turning, I'd just write a stream of consciousness,' Waits recalls, 'and then sift through and find something to use.'[6] Melodies were dismantled, lyrics discarded and pieces of songs rearranged until they fitted together, generating more than twelve different songs to be used wherever they were required. Unlike the usual process followed when composing a film score, it was impossible for Waits to write the songs in sequence with the film since it was never known when the script was going to change or where the songs would be placed. Once shooting began, Waits looked to the film for direction, but even this proved to be unreliable as scenes were constantly chopped and changed. Finally, Waits resigned himself to following Coppola's original suggestion: write anything and a place will be found for it.[7] A sense of how loose the composition process was at times is given in an anecdote that recalls how a visitor to the set completed the lyrics to one of Waits's songs. Sung by the Latin character played by Raul Julia, the lyrics to 'It's Raining Cuban Cigars' were contributed by none other than Gene Kelly – apt, given his 'Singin' in the Rain' scene from the 1952 musical of the same name.[8] With only a title and melody, Waits was stuck for appropriate lyrics when Kelly heard the opening line. Waits recalls telling him to '"give me a beautiful lyric," and Gene wrote one.'[9] Making only the briefest appearance in the film, the song was never fleshed out and so didn't make it onto the LP.

Bob Alcivar worked closely with Waits on the arrangement for each of the songs, scoring them, variously, for a small jazz combo, a big-band sound and symphonically, for orchestra. Over the course of the following months, they built up as much as six hours of music, the earliest songs of which were recorded in October, six months after Waits began work on the film. For the trio and quartet numbers, a team of veteran players from the glory years of West Coast 1950s jazz were assembled. Bassist Greg Cohen was joined by pianist Pete Jolly, drummer Shelly Manne, trumpeter Jack Sheldon and Teddy Edwards on tenor sax. Typified by 'Picking Up After You', five of the songs were conceived as duets with country singer Crystal Gayle, three of them, including 'Is There Any Way Out of this Dream?' featuring only her voice, and four of them – 'I Beg Your Pardon', 'Little Boy Blue', 'You Can't Unring a Bell' and 'Broken Bicycles' – being solo vehicles for Waits. Fully orchestrated instrumental montages filled out the soundtrack. The overall impression was not so different to Sinatra and Riddle's *Pal Joey* soundtrack.

Needing a contrast to the relatively glacial pace of work on the film, in June 1980 Waits forsook the office on the Zoetrope lot and temporarily moved into the studio in the RCA Building on Ivar and Sunset in Hollywood to make *Heartattack and Vine*. Working at quite a clip, Waits was writing a song a night, handing it off to arranger Bones Howe the next morning and then recording it in the afternoon. Once a track on the LP was finished, the process began again – the idea being to complete a new song every night so that when the band arrived there would be something fresh for them to work on. 'I mean I used to hear everything with upright bass, muted trumpet, or tenor sax,' reflects Waits: 'I just sort of had a limited musical scope, so I wanted to try to stretch out a little bit on the new one.'[10] The concentrated bluesy feel of the LP – with Roland Bautista's lead guitar and Ronnie Barron's Hammond organ, underpinned by the rhythm section of John Thomassie, drummer for blues legend Freddie King, and Larry Taylor, bass player for psychedelic blues outfit Canned Heat – gives a sense of the intensity of the writing and recording process. Along with 'Downtown', "Til The Money Runs Out' and 'In Shades', 'Heartattack and Vine' finds Waits at his most edgy so far. 'The title track was a breakthrough for me,' confirms Waits, 'using that kind of Yardbirds fuzz guitar, having the drummer use sticks instead of brushes.'[11] The lyrics on the title track are some of his most hard-boiled to date, typified by the couplet about there not being a Devil, just a drunken God. This new development provided Waits with what he refers to as a 'tunnel to laterally make some kind of transition' to a different sound, a point reached two years later with *Swordfishtrombones*.[12] For now, however, the complete transition, based on a new, harsher type of crooning, would have to wait.

Lyrically, most of the songs on *Heartattack and Vine* occupy the noir territory typified by Raymond Chandler's *The Long Goodbye* (1953), albeit via the new journalism of Hunter S. Thompson, which lent it a gonzo twist. Bearing the influence of the arrangements from *One from the Heart*, while the ballads 'Jersey Girl' and 'On the Nickel' from *Heartattack and Vine* receive Alcivar's full orchestral treatment, the final track on Side 2, 'Ruby's Arms', is the lushest, with Jerry Yester's imprudently ladled-on strings belying their rapid orchestration. Of the latter, Waits comments: 'I love Jerry's arrangement on it. He used a brass choir and made it sound like a Salvation Army band at the top of the tune.'[13] 'It's a little bit like that Matt Monro thing, "I Will Leave You Softly",' says Waits, referring to Monro's version of 'Softly, As I Leave You' from 1962.[14] Sinatra actually covered the tune in 1964 – even naming an entire Reprise LP after it – but added little to Monro's interpretation, which likely accounts for why Waits recalls the English singer's version of the song. When writing the lyrics, Waits tells of 'trying to visualise this guy getting up in the morning before dawn and leaving on the train, with the clothesline outside'.[15] Widely assumed to be about the end of Waits's relationship with singer Rickie Lee Jones, 'Ruby's Arms' includes a lyric that revolves around the protagonist's heart breaking as he steals away before his partner wakes. Written by Tony De Vita and Giorgio Calabrese in 1960, and later given an English lyric by Hal Shaper, Monro's recording of 'Softly, As I Leave You' emphasizes the lyrics detailing how the protagonist's heart will be broken should his exit be noticed. Perversely, the Salvation Army-esque brass of 'Ruby's Arms' gives the schmaltz of the strings an edge, and – together with Waits in his deepest, most gravel-laden voice – strike a poignant, almost cloying note. Waits's underpinning of 'Ruby's Arms' with the schmaltz of Monro's 'Softly, As I Leave You' lends the track a sense of camp. Susan Sontag asks 'why so many of the objects prized by Camp taste are old-fashioned, out-of-date, *démodé*.' 'It's not', she continues, 'a love of the old as such . . . [but] that the process of ageing . . . arouses a necessary sympathy.'[16] The example Sontag provides to illustrate her point could not be more apt. 'Many people who listen with delight to the style of Rudy Vallée revived by the English pop group the Temperance Seven, would have been driven up the wall by Rudy Vallée in his heyday.'[17] In 1980, a hit by an English crooner, Monro, from his heyday in the early 1960s provides Waits with the desired sentiment. Using 'Softly, As I Leave You' as a touchstone, with 'Ruby's Arms', Waits writes a contemporary torch ballad that locates the emotive moment in a break-up not in retrospect, as is the norm, but in the recognition of the break-up in the eyes of the other. Bringing the emotive moment forward like this gives the listener the voyeuristic sense of experiencing something while it is still playing out. The listener is there with Waits as he croons about stealing away in the early morning light, taking Ruby's scarf off the clothesline on the way.

Once *Heartattack and Vine* was completed, Waits made his way back to Zoetrope and the soundtrack, but his return was not without tension. The singer found it 'a little difficult . . . to resume writing music that wasn't a little gnarled and driving – the kind of stuff I was writing for *Heartattack and Vine*'.[18] But the experience of having made *Heartattack and Vine* before being forced to return to *One from the Heart* actually benefitted the soundtrack, in one instance causing Waits to reject the fully orchestrated version of 'Broken Bicycles' already cut – far more in keeping with the nature of the rest of the LP – in favour of a sparser demo version. In this sense, the two very different LPs – *One from the Heart* and *Heartattack and Vine* – feed into each other. The sparseness of 'Broken Bicycles' means it would fit more readily on *Heartattack and Vine*, and the lushness of 'Ruby's Arms' means it would not sound out of place on *One from the Heart*. Of 'Broken Bicycles', from the former LP, Bones Howe recalls:

> [The song] in the film is, in fact, a two-track demo of Tom singing and playing piano, and Greg [Cohen] playing upright bass. It was done at the end of a session where we had recorded other music, and Tom said, 'Let me get this down on tape so I can listen to it.' We didn't even bother to make a 24-track of it because we assumed it would be re-recorded with a huge string section later, which in fact it was. But we ended up using the original two-track because with the big string section it ended up sounding too dramatic.[19]

Knowing the demo version of 'Broken Bicycles' was more effective for being sparser, Howe and Waits used it as the final track on Side 1 of the LP. The brief opening piano motif presages Waits's vocal entrance. Midway through the verse, Cohen enters on bass, filling out the sound and lending it a slow swing. The last verse of the song includes some of Waits's most intimate singing, with the final lines finding Waits's voice reduced to just a hoarse whisper. In a reversal characteristic of *One from the Heart*'s production, after hearing 'Broken Bicycles', Coppola wrote a scene to accompany it, which became one of the film's most memorable moments. The film's male lead owns a wrecking yard for abandoned cars and is

forced to sell a prized Studebaker, breaking his heart in the process. 'So I came up with this idea for a used car lot piece,' Waits explains, 'where the music is conducted with a dipstick.'[20] While the scene is rich in atmosphere, it's also one of the most obscure in the film.

Until this point (1980–81), the 1950s remained the defining decade for Waits's crooning and the thematic approach to putting an LP together. The 1950s leaves its print on *One from the Heart* via the musicals of the decade, while *Heartattack and Vine* is shot through with the narrative settings of Chandler's novel *The Long Goodbye*. Waits's voice on both LPs bears the melodic sensibility of Hoagy Carmichael's late recordings from the 1950s, and the mature voice that Louis Armstrong developed during the same decade.

The facility to coordinate together romantic ballads, bluesy jives and laid-back cocktail songs on both Waits LPs betrays the influence of Carmichael's ability to effortlessly move between the nostalgic romanticism of 'Stardust', the idyllic drawl of 'Georgia on My Mind' and the humour of 'Hong Kong Blues'. Even more than the original recordings, made at the time the songs were written in the 1920s and '30s, the songs' reimagining via arranger Johnny Mandel on *Hoagy Sings Carmichael: With the Pacific Jazzmen and Conducted by Johnny Mandel* (1957) is especially appropriate to Waits. '[Carmichael] didn't try to be a capital-S singer,' says Mandel of *Hoagy Sings Carmichael: With the Pacific Jazzmen and Conducted by Johnny Mandel*, and 'more often he approached the songs conversationally, like an actor, like Walter Huston.'[21] Correspondences between Carmichael's LP, Waits and Sinatra abound. Featured altoist Art Pepper is from the same generation and school as Waits's preferred drummer Shelly Manne on the *One from the Heart* soundtrack, and featured trumpeter Harry Edison appears throughout Sinatra's Mandel-arranged *Ring a Ding Ding!* (1961). Working together within Mandel's orchestrations,

Hoagy Carmichael (1899–1981), u.s. pianist, composer and film actor.

Carmichael and the sidemen embrace 'New Orleans', 'Winter Moon' and 'Rockin Chair', all titles Waits would appropriate in the 1970s, with 'I Wish I Was in New Orleans' from *Small Change* (1976), 'Grapefruit Moon' from *Closing Time* (1973) and 'Rockin' Chair' (1971), respectively. If the diversity of Waits's songwriting and instrumentation bears the influence of Carmichael's passage through 1950s cool jazz, then his style of crooning very much comes from the Armstrong of the same period. Where Armstrong's vocals on the hot fives from the 1920s feature scat singing, by the 1950s Armstrong's vocal approach had eased in pace and broadened in vibrato. LPs of the decade, particularly *Louis Armstrong Meets Oscar Peterson* (1957), find Armstrong with a newly realized depth of tone, interpreting the songs of Johnny Mercer and others. Armstrong's sustained vibrato on 'What's New?' cracks into a hoarse whisper, a technique Waits makes use of throughout his ballad singing and especially on 'Broken Bicycles' and 'Ruby's Arms'. Used too frequently, this can become bathetic, but if used judiciously it can be extremely effective. Vocally, it is late Armstrong more than Captain Beefheart that makes its way into Waits's crooning at this point, the widely assumed Beefheart influence only becoming apparent with *Swordfishtrombones* two years later.[22]

In addition to Chandler, in interviews Waits often notes the importance of Jack Kerouac's writings from the 1950s. The LP Kerouac and musician Steve Allen made together in 1959 of the former reciting streams of poetry over the latter's improvised piano chordings is particularly pertinent. 'The first time I heard any spoken word that I was really impressed with was an album called *Jack Kerouac/Steve Allen*,' says Waits, '[and] it was real, real effective.'[23] In fact, the main reason Waits chose to collaborate with Howe was less because of his music credentials and more to do with the producer's work on another Kerouac spoken-word LP. Although Kerouac is usually associated with the be-bop jazz of Thelonious Monk and Charlie Parker – their endless impassioned staccato solos finding

Louis Armstrong performing live, date unknown.

their equivalence in Kerouac's stream-of-consciousness writing style – Sinatra's torch ballads also had an often-overlooked presence in the Beat poet's writing. By no coincidence, when polled by Leonard Feather in 1956 for the *Encyclopaedia Yearbook of Jazz* who their favourite singer was, bebop pianist Bud Powell and trumpeter Miles

Publicity photo of American musician Tom Waits, c. 1974–5.

Davis overwhelmingly chose Sinatra.[24] Though styled on be-bop, Kerouac's *Big Sur* (1961) contains numerous references to Sinatra's *No One Cares* (1959), the singer's latest LP of torch ballads at the time. 'The goddamned last gory detail of some dismal robbery of the heart at dawn,' writes Kerouac, 'when no one cares like Sinatra sings.'[25] The song 'A Cottage for Sale' on the *No One Cares* LP recounts precisely that 'dismal robbery of the heart at dawn' as it narrates the need to sell a property following the end of a relationship. Anchored by his crooning, both 'Ruby's Arms' and 'Broken Bicycles' find Waits extending this mood and metaphor.

In addition to turning away from the music of his contemporaries of the early 1970s typified by LA singer-songwriters such as Jackson Browne, Waits seldom engaged in the music of the previous decade either. Commenting on a lack of interest in the musical landscape of the 1960s, Waits recalls 'listening to Sinatra when I was starting out. My friends thought I was crazy.'[26] From *The Heart of Saturday Night* onwards, Waits actually responds to Sinatra in a number of ways. 'It's kind of like you start imitating the things that are around you, whatever they are,' Waits explains, '[and] I took note of Frank Sinatra. I liked the scar on the side of his face,' Waits notes: '[Sinatra] had this tremendous birthmark that he was always careful to obscure in photographs, but I saw one photo that showed this – it almost looked like a burn on the side of his face.'[27] Waits may be referring to a picture published in *Life* magazine in April 1965, which captures Sinatra in a sauna, wrapped in a towel, with the birthmark clearly visible. Birthmarks aside, visually Waits first feeds Sinatra in through the artwork on *The Heart of Saturday Night*, featuring an illustration of Waits in a suit standing alone by a lamppost at night, close in feel and composition to Sinatra's iconic *In the Wee Small Hours* cover. While shorter-brimmed and Monk-like, the fedora Waits began wearing in the late 1970s in both photography shoots and live performances is a further gesture in Sinatra's direction.

Waits's crooning changes subtly at first, between early demos informally recorded in 1971, the debut LP *Closing Time* (1973) and *The Heart of Saturday Night* (1974). The change then becomes dramatic on *Nighthawks at the Diner* (1975) and *Small Change* (1976). Part of the reason for this emphatic change in late 1974 is apparently circumstantial, the result of the nightly strain on his voice as Waits battled to be heard against constant heckling when touring with labelmate Frank Zappa in the autumn of that year. At first, Waits was concerned enough about it to consult none other than Sinatra's doctor, but then realized that the damage could be put to use by creating a character out of the voice.[28] 'During that period, it was like going to a costume party and coming home without changing,' observes Waits: 'I really became a character in my own story. I'd go out at night, get drunk, fall asleep underneath a car. Come home . . . bang my head on the piano and somehow chronicle my own demise.'[29] Damaged as an instrument, the voice as person and the voice as character are blurred by Waits to pilot a distinctive type of crooning that is refined on both *Heartattack and Vine* and *One from the Heart*.

Francis Thumm, a classically trained pianist who would play a key collaborative role in Waits's later music, recalls how in the early 1970s the pair would sit at the piano and reel off songs by the Doors in the style of Sinatra, Thumm's favourite being 'Tom singing "Riders on the Storm".'[30] Tellingly, for a song from a late 1960s/early 1970s group to attract Waits in this way, it had to be funnelled through a singer associated with the 1950s. If 'Broken Bicycles' feels very like the 1950s update of Carmichael found on the LP *Hoagy Sings Carmichael: With the Pacific Jazzmen and Conducted by Johnny Mandel*, then 'Ruby's Arms' is perhaps best thought of less in terms of late Armstrong and more in line with what Sinatra singing 'Riders on the Storm' might have sounded like. With the turn into the 1980s, Waits actually attempted to feed Sinatra new songs in the hope of them being covered. While it never came to pass, it's not too much of a stretch to assume that this is precisely what Waits is reaching for on ballads of this period. 'Why don't you pretend I'm Frank Sinatra and write what Nelson Riddle would write?', Waits growled to one of his arrangers.[31] With his Altec 21D as the vocal mic of choice – precisely 'because Sinatra used it' in live performances – Waits's crooning almost does sound like Sinatra singing 'Riders on the Storm'.[32]

Grace Jones in Los Angeles, 8 July 1984.

7

Grace Jones:
'Unlimited Capacity for Love' (1982)

The scene is Compass Point studios, Nassau, in late 1979, and Grace Jones has just started recording the first instalment of her Compass Point Trilogy: *Warm Leatherette* (1980), *Nightclubbing* (1981) and *Living My Life* (1982). The significance of the LP trilogy lies in the way Jones adopts both the deeper voice and visual cues of the male crooner. Appropriately, the cover of *Nightclubbing* shows Jones wearing a suit jacket and smoking a cigarette, akin to the covers of Frank Sinatra's *In the Wee Small Hours* (1955), Bryan Ferry's *Another Time, Another Place* (1974) and Tom Waits's *The Heart of Saturday Night* (1974). The Compass Point Trilogy crosses borders between musical genres by skilfully fusing reggae, electro pop and new wave, causing Jones to refer to it as a 'stylized border crossing . . . [blending] reggae, electronics, [and] pop'.[1] Earlier fusions between jazz, rock and reggae seldom yielded musical works as economical as the Compass Point Trilogy. Pressing against racial and gender stereotypes while simultaneously crossing the borders of numerous musical genres, Jones's Compass Point Trilogy lends further ballast to how the crooner operates at the progressive edge of popular music.

The Compass Point Trilogy is the first time the output of a crooner is totally premised on the collaboration of the vocalist with a producer and musicians from the songwriting upwards. For the first recording session in late 1979, Jones and her co-producer, Island

Records founder Chris Blackwell, arranged for the musicians – principally, Sly Dunbar on bass, Robbie Shakespeare on drums, Barry Reynolds and Michael Chung on guitar, Wally Badarou on keyboards and Uziah 'Sticky' Thompson on percussion – to arrive a few days early, in order to become familiar with one another. After a few days bedding in, the musicians' extensive chops lead to them producing a series of sleek sonic collages. By example, Shakespeare's reggae bass propelling 'Pull Up to the Bumper' is constantly caressed by Reynolds's funky guitar riff, and stabs from Badarou's keyboard that seem to interrupt the groove actually serve to accentuate it. What Jones refers to as her 'stylized border crossing' of musical genres causes there to be, according to Blackwell, 'a tension between each faction in the group', with the European new wave and pop musicians on one side, and the Jamaican reggae-based musicians on the other.[2] The musicians immediately sensed the purpose behind Jones and Blackwell's approach, with Badarou acknowledging how it lent 'the music dissonance', making it more engaging.[3] Achieved through collaboration, and premised on the notion of creating a border crossing as a bed for the the deeper voice of the crooner to lie on, each track on Jones's Compass Point Trilogy finds a fresh way to articulate this dissonance.

Seemingly in tension with the sensibility of the crooner, the passage of reggae into new wave via punk constitutes the immediate context for the collaborative instrumental aspects of the Compass Point Trilogy. 'I knew that I liked reggae and I wanted to mix it in using a more aggressive sound,' says Jones, referring to the infusion of punk and new wave into reggae.[4] Based on their shared drive to raise political consciousness, the relationship between punk and reggae was piloted by the Clash on '(White Man) in Hammersmith

New York, 1981: Jamaican-born singer, fashion model and actress Grace Jones performs onstage during a concert at the Savoy Club. The androgynous Jones, a cult favourite among the gay and disco crowd, had a number of hits including 'Warm Leatherette' and 'Pull Up to the Bumper'.

Palais' (1977) and the band's Lee Scratch Perry-produced single 'Complete Control' (1977). As punk opened out onto new wave, the fascination with reggae deepened, with 'Attack' from PiL's *Public Image (First Issue)* (1978) bringing sonic elements of reggae into collision with new wave, a tendency enhanced on the band's *Metal Box* (1979). Broadening new wave's fascination with reggae to incorporate funk, Talking Heads' 'Once in a Lifetime' from *Remain in Light* (1980) – partially recorded at Compass Point – uses a hypnotic reggae-derived bass riff as a focal point, causing its producer, one-time Roxy Music member Brian Eno, to describe how the 'song has a funny balance, with two centres of gravity – their funk groove, and my dubby, reggae-ish understanding of it'.[5] The passage of reggae into new wave via punk lent the Compass Point Trilogy a 'more aggressive sound', as Jones desired, and ensured that there would be a tension in her twisting of the crooner archetype.

Jones's premising her version of the crooner on a stylized border crossing meant that the sensibilities of each of the musicians contributing to the Compass Point Trilogy was crucial. Where other crooners need only a simple guitar or piano to compose, or the accompaniment of a single acoustic instrument to sing, Jones required the input of each of the musicians assembled in the studio in Nassau to generate the music. In this sense, more than any of the other crooners detailed in the previous chapters, collaboration is vital to Jones. Consequently, the make-up of Jones's band, the Compass Point Allstars that appear on the trilogy, plays a prominent role.

The Compass Point Trilogy is underpinned by Jamaica's crack rhythm section, Dunbar and Shakespeare. Used to collaborating with vocalists, the duo came to Jones fresh from working on Black Uhuru's *Showcase* (1979), Serge Gainsbourg's *Aux armes et caetera* (1979) and Peter Tosh's *Mystic Man* (1979). Where on *Showcase* Dunbar and Shakespeare collaborated with Black Uhuru to develop a leaner type of reggae, on 'Buk-In-Hamm Palace' from Tosh's *Mystic Man* the duo fashioned a more percussive sound, with Shakespeare's drumming patterns heightened by Jamaican 'Sticky' Thompson's percussion. Dunbar commented on how, with their input, Tosh the militant reggae artist 'came off like disco'.[6] With the duo's help, Jones, the disco singer, would come off like reggae.

British songwriter and guitarist Barry Reynolds not only contributed his spiky, new-wave guitar playing but worked closely with Jones to compose songs throughout the Compass Point Trilogy. Reynolds arrived at Compass Point direct from playing on Marianne Faithfull's new-wave breakthrough *Broken English*, released by Island Records in 1979. 'There was something I did on this track called "Why'd You Do It",' explains Reynolds, 'a mix of heavy roots reggae with a European edge to it', which triggered the invitation to Nassau.[7] 'Why'd You Do It' is indeed a perfect melding of heavy reggae rhythm and angular lead. Contrasting with the way the Compass Point All-stars' other guitarist, Chinese Jamaican Michael Chung, locks in rhythmically with Dunbar and Shakespeare, Reynolds's hard-edged guitar licks pepper the track 'Private Life' from *Warm Leatherette*, lending the music a spikiness.

French African keyboardist Wally Badarou brings a crucial electro-pop sensibility to the Compass Point Trilogy. 'When we all landed in Nassau,' recalls Badarou – who Blackwell had heard on M's 'Pop Muzik' (1979) – 'Barry and I were curious about Sly, Robbie, Mickey and Sticky's ability to play disco music, while they were questioning our ability to play reggae.'[8] Once they got into the studio, however, 'things just unfolded, no questions asked.'[9] *Warm Leatherette* was the first time Badarou appeared on more rhythmic-based groove music, lending the trilogy an electro-pop dimension crucial to the border crossing Jones was striving for.[10]

By moving between the spoken voice and the sung voice on the trilogy, Jones makes the most unexpected contribution to the crooner archetype to date. Where Barry White tended to position spoken-word segments at the beginning of a song, on 'Walking in the Rain' from *Nightclubbing*, Jones carries it all the way through.[11]

Marlene Dietrich, 'Morocco', 1930.

'Once I started singing along with the heavy bass and machine-gun drum of Sly and Robbie it was actually an advantage that I had the voice I did,' insists Jones: 'there was no space for a standard soul or funk voice in that sound.'[12] She describes her newfound voice of late 1979 as being 'somewhere between half-speaking and half-singing'.[13] The notion of 'half-speaking' suggests that both proto and early rap were crucial for Jones. The Sugar Hill Gang's 'Rapper's Delight' released in the autumn of 1979 provides the immediate contemporary context for Jones's vocal treatment on tracks such as 'Private Life', which was cut just a few months later. So too does Serge Gainsbourg's *Aux armes et cœtera*, recorded in Kingston, Jamaica, in early 1979 using not only Dunbar and Shakespeare but Thompson and Chung. The recording accentuated the already rap-like elements of Jones's vocal delivery by stripping back the sound to emphasize drum and bass.

Jones's deep voice established a continuity with the crooner archetype, and freed her up to embrace new musical genres such as new wave and rap, the latter associated with deeper-voiced male vocalists. In her memoir *I'll Never Write My Memoirs* (2015), Jones recalls the significance of speaking to a pioneer of the recorded low-voiced female vocalist, Marlene Dietrich, by phone: 'I said, "Hello," in my usual deep voice. And she said, "Well, you sound just like me" . . . It was like we were in a little club of deep, manly speakers.'[14] The cabaret-crooner archetype Dietrich piloted in the 1930s, and played through to even greater effect in various live performances in the late 1960s and early 1970s – captured in the film with David Bowie, *Just a Gigolo* (1978) – provides an important precedent for Jones. 'Now that I had lowered my voice I didn't need anything sweet around me,' affirms Jones: 'I had made a decision not to try to be like the gospel-tinged female singers I admired. There were male singers I loved that perhaps made more sense: . . . Bobby Womack, and, of course, Barry White.'[15] With no contemporary female singers in a register as low as Dietrich, it's understandable that Jones reached for Barry White when searching for a vocal touchstone. In 1977, Jones picked up where White had left off and piloted a funk-laced form of disco that left her with ample capacity to continue developing her sound into the early 1980s. Although the bass-baritone register of White's voice was technically out of reach, Jones still developed one of the lowest female voices in contemporary popular music, and had a desire to learn more about it: 'I was a student of my own voice, and a part of that learning was to get to like my voice. I never liked that people thought I was a man, how they thought my voice sounded too low and monotonous. I learned that this was my voice.'[16]

With the aim of contrasting Jones's voice with both past crooners like Sinatra and contemporary crooners typified by White, Bowie and Ferry, producer Tom Moulton insisted during Jone's disco years (1977–9) on using a vocal coach to train Jones to sing in a higher register akin to popular female vocalists of the time, such as Diana Ross and Donna Summer. This period yielded three LPS – *Portfolio* (1977), *Fame* (1978) and *Muse* (1979) – all recorded at Sigma Sound Studios in Philadelphia. Jones bemoaned how the LPS were all Moulton's vision, following 'the same formula . . . the glossy, tightly arranged Philly frills' that Bowie used to great effect on his unreleased LP *The Gouster* (1975), an early version of what became *Young Americans* (1975).[17] Realizing that the voice that had developed on the disco LPS was not distinctive enough, Jones eventually rejected the instruction of the voice coach: 'I was very undisciplined about that and they threatened to tear up my contract. But I thought it was ridiculous people trying to teach me how to *breathe*. I learnt how to breathe when I was born!'[18] The idea of swimming laps underwater to increase lung capacity, as Sinatra did, was evidently not only unattractive but inappropriate to the distinctive vocal style Jones was to aim for a few years later on the Compass Point Trilogy.

Nowhere does Jones mention Tosh in interviews or her auto-biography, even though it can be argued that the one-time Wailer is uniquely important to Jones for having one of the few baritone voices in reggae. Initially cut for the Perry-produced Wailers LP *Soul Rebels* (1970), the track '400 Years' is the first to showcase Tosh's distinctive voice. The song was remade for the band's debut LP on Island Records, *Catch a Fire* (1973), with the enhanced clarity of the production capturing the timbre of Tosh's voice more effectively. The Wailers' second LP on Island, *Burnin'* (1973), includes the track 'Small Axe', which features Tosh on backing vocals to great effect, uttering a phrase in the chorus at one of the lowest baritones ever recorded in reggae, providing the track with a well-defined bottom end. Leaving the Wailers and working with Dunbar and Shakespeare, from *Equal Rights* (1977) onwards, Tosh sought more creative room for his voice. The baritone quality of Tosh's voice guides the one Jones developed on the Compass Point Trilogy.

In terms of other contemporary female vocalists providing an alternative to what Jones refers to as the 'standard soul or funk voice', Nina Simone is perhaps the only contemporary female crooner of the time to call on the reggae genre. The reggae-inflected LP *Baltimore* (1978), recorded for producer Creed Taylor's label CTI the year before Jones and Blackwell assembled the Compass Point Allstars, is a key precedent for the Compass Point Trilogy. Simone's deep voice – alternating between the almost spoken nature of the terse verses and the smoothly sung choruses, floating over the reggae groove of the LP's title track, written by Randy Newman – contrasts sharply with the voice of not only contemporary soul singers typified by Aretha Franklin but Jamaican reggae vocalists such as Marcia Griffiths.

Only with the second and third instalments of the Compass Point Trilogy – *Nightclubbing* and *Living My Life* – do Jones's self-penned songs play a more significant role in the retooling of the crooner archetype. The first instalment, *Warm Leatherette*, includes only one self-penned song, 'A Rolling Stone'; the rest are cover versions. Jones and Blackwell selected the songs to cover together, either from recent crooners such as Ferry, Bowie and Iggy Pop, or from new-wave acts registering their influence, including Joy Division and the Normal. As Jones describes, 'Chris [Blackwell] and his team brought in songs that were unusual . . . to suit our new approach. Nothing that was as obvious as the show tunes, perhaps, but in many ways, new forms of show tunes. New-wave show tunes, Iggy Pop as the new Frank Sinatra.'[19]

The idea of 'Iggy Pop as the new Frank Sinatra' reveals how Jones was approaching both the selection of material and its vocal treatment in terms of the history of the crooner. Though rock based, as with Ferry and Bowie, Iggy Pop recast the make-up of the crooner throughout the 1970s, especially on tracks such as 'Tonight' (1977). Speaking about the LP *Only the Lonely* (1958), Iggy Pop revealed a fascination with what he characterized as Sinatra's '"otherworldly" phrasing'.[20] By covering songs by these three figures – Ferry, Bowie and Pop – Jones accesses the lineage of the crooner without having to go all the way back to Sinatra. Jones's version of Ferry's 'Love Is the Drug' (1975) appears on *Warm Leatherette*, while Bowie and Iggy Pop's 'Nightclubbing' (1977) is covered on the Compass Point Trilogy's second instalment. With Dunbar and Shakespeare easing the rhythm towards reggae, Jones accentuates the already prominent role given to the beat in the original versions. Songs written by new-wave artists on the Compass Point Trilogy include Joy Division's 'She's Lost Control', fresh from the band's first LP *Unknown Pleasures* (1979) and placed on the B side of Jones's 'Private Life' single, with the heavy electronic drum beat of the original

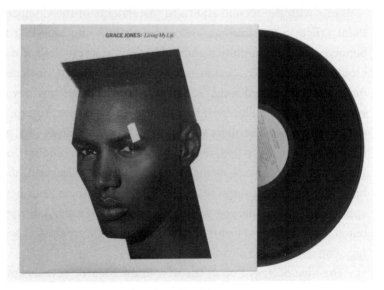

Grace Jones, *Living My Life* album cover (1982).

being, like 'Nightclubbing', accentuated. In this sense, both Iggy Pop and Ian Curtis serve as 'the new Frank Sinatra' for Jones.

Underlining their importance to Jones's reworking of the crooner archetype, self-penned songs develop in quantity, from one on *Warm Leatherette* to three on *Nightclubbing* and six on *Living My Life*. With the last, these tracks represent all but one song on the LP, spotlighting how Jones was becoming an increasingly prolific songwriter. 'Grace had never really written songs before,' explains guitarist Barry Reynolds, accounting for the slow start, 'so we started writing together.'[21] Reynolds continues:

> We wrote 'Art Groupie' as she was splitting up with Jean-Paul [Goude]. And one of the reasons for the song's direction was how much Jean-Paul was into the art scene . . . She just gave me these lyrics written on a piece of paper and I took them home and put it together.[22]

Jones would also write with Shakespeare and Dunbar, but the majority of her self-penned songs for the Compass Point Trilogy were written in collaboration with Reynolds, who at the same time was working on his solo LP for Island, *I Scare Myself*, cut using the Compass Point Allstars in Nassau. Co-written by Jones and Reynolds, 'Unlimited Capacity For Love' comes from the often-overlooked third instalment of the Compass Point Trilogy, *Living My Life*, released in November 1982. With the exception of the first track of Side 1, 'My Jamaican Guy', the LP is much less accessible than *Warm Leatherette* or *Nightclubbing*. As a context for the torch ballad 'Unlimited Capacity For Love', Jones's *Living My Life* finds her close to what Eno calls a 'dubby, reggae-ish' take on the funk groove underpinning numerous tracks on Talking Heads' *Remain in Light* (1980).[23] Across *Living My Life* the atmosphere is colder, the groove less joyous, even though each song seems to be a more personal statement. Tracks such as the penultimate one on Side 2, 'Inspiration', feel emotionally taut, and the title track was actually left off the finished LP as it was deemed too downbeat. 'Unlimited Capacity for Love' is the final track on Side 2 of the LP and therefore the conclusion of the entire Compass Point Trilogy. The song comments on the cultural ability to continue loving in the face of emotional extremes. More than just another torch ballad, it is a reflection on the social patterns that trigger these songs in the first place. A torch ballad about torch ballads. This approach adds an additional meta layer to the equation, complementing the way Jones accesses the crooner via Iggy Pop and Ian Curtis without recourse to Sinatra. Each verse of 'Unlimited Capacity for Love' is sung in what, for Jones, is a relatively higher-pitched voice, reminiscent of the typical female soul singers Jones was so keen to distance herself from. Contrasting with this, the chorus – which consists of the title refrain repeated – is sung in Jones's usual low register. The second time the chorus appears, it is echoed by what sounds like a voice treated with a vocoder, exaggerating the already-robotic way Jones sings the line containing the title phrase, numbing its emotive power. Jones and Chris Blackwell would certainly have been familiar with Laurie Anderson's 'O Superman' (1981) when cutting the track in 1982, using the vocoder in a more sensitive way, probably via an Eventide Harmonizer as Kraftwerk had done on 'Ohm Sweet Ohm' (1975). This torch song about torch songs, written by Jones and Reynolds, undoes the sentimentality/sensuality binary typically structuring the genre by refusing to yield to any aspect of sentimentality.

At the point of arriving in Nassau in late 1979 to work with Jones, Reynolds was more accustomed to writing with Marianne Faithfull. At Blackwell's invitation, Faithfull attended the recording of 'I've Done It Again', unaware that the song, co-written by her, had been gifted to Jones. Reynolds recalls how, listening in the corner of the studio, '[Marianne] goes to me, "We wrote that!"'[24] But earlier in 1979 Faithfull had rejected the song, claiming it was 'too jazzy'.[25] Like the crooners Bowie, Ferry and Pop, Faithfull was a figure from an earlier moment reinvigorated by punk. Where in Bowie's case this led to the Berlin trilogy (1977–9), with Ferry it resulted in Roxy Music's *Manifesto* (1979), both, in turn, feeding back into the contemporary and influencing successive moments of new wave typified by Japan's *Gentlemen Take Polaroids* (1980), an LP shot through with David Sylvian's crooning. Faithfull is the only female songwriter besides Chrissie Hynde whom Jones draws on for the Compass Point Trilogy.[26]

As with Jones's recording of a Faithfull song, the nature of the lyrics – in cover versions and self-penned songs – plays a fundamental role in the way Jones fashions her persona by reconstructing the crooner archetype. 'We were looking for something unpredictable . . . that reflects my attitude lyric-wise,' Jones explains, finding it in the 'whole new attitude in the lyrics [written] from a woman's point of view'.[27] Disparagingly, Jones describes how, prior to punk and new wave, 'usually you end up with women singing, "You can go and cheat on me but . . . I'll love you if you come home."'[28] While Jones's cover versions of songs such as 'I've Done It Again' – featuring Faithfull's lyrics – articulate this point of view, her self-penned songs convey it even more forcefully. Jones's drive to be a new type of crooner required the new type of lyric that we find honed on 'Unlimited Capacity for Love'.

Spotlighting the role played by collaboration in Jones's retooling of the crooner archetype, Blackwell suggested that the musicians rehearse first and then go into the studio, but 'Robbie said, "No, go into the studio and record everything we rehearse."'[29] That way, each moment of the collaboration would be captured at its freshest. Aided by engineer and co-producer Alex Sadkin, 'the first tune recorded was "Warm Leatherette",' says Dunbar, 'and I heard it played back and [thought] "Wow!"' Then, the second one was 'Private Life'.[30] In a two-week period they cut over thirty tracks. 'We recorded from scratch, as live as possible . . . and needed someone fantastically fluent at mixing on the go, to capture the groove as it was happening,' says Sadkin, reflecting on his multiple roles as engineer, co-mixer and co-producer.[31] 'The Jamaican musicians were incredibly tight,' says Reynolds, 'we would do two takes of something at the most and then Robbie . . . [would] say, "Yeah, we good with this one let's move on!"'[32] Dunbar describes how 'Grace felt the most at home, I think, at Compass Point,' and 'being in Nassau with us, the ocean is there, she was always relaxed and ready to work when she came down'.[33] The sympathetic atmosphere of both the place and the musicians left Jones free to focus on her vocals and songwriting. '[Compass Point] was the first time I really worked with somebody – not just going into the studio, putting on headphones and singing to tracks. Everyone worked very closely together.'[34] Dunbar explains having to initially 'lay the rhythm down and then hum the melody' to songs to Jones until they were familiar.[35] This process gradually changed from 1979 to 1982 as Jones's creative remit widened beyond just her voice and the selection of musicians to encompass songwriting. To begin with providing only the lyrics and being reliant on either Shakespeare, Dunbar or Reynolds for the song structure and melody, by the time of 'Unlimited Capacity for Love', Jones was contributing to structure and melody too.

It is little wonder that Jones conceived of Iggy Pop and others as the new Sinatra in the early 1980s because whenever attempts were made to update the archetypical crooner's sound in this period, the results were desultory. Following Sinatra's attempts at disco in 1977, the Quincy Jones-produced LP LA Is My Lady (1984) by Sinatra blends together electro-pop and jazz. Though a number of the LP's tracks are reworkings of classics from the American Songbook, the new title track by Alan and Marilyn Bergman is the most contemporary sounding, with both daubs of synthesizer played by Craig Huxley and organ played by Jimmy Smith counterpointing George Benson's funky guitar licks. Listening to Jones's 'Unlimited Capacity for Love' and 'LA Is My Lady' back-to-back spotlights just how out of sync with the times Sinatra was by 1984.

The stylized sonic border crossing that underpinned Jones's retooling of the crooner archetype on the Compass Point Trilogy dynamically opens out onto broader questions of gender and race. For Jones, its complexity is encapsulated in a detail as apparently simple as her haircut: 'My shaved head made me look more abstract, less tied to a specific race or sex or tribe, but was also a way of moving across those things . . . I was black, but not black; woman, but not woman; American, but Jamaican; African, but science fiction.'[36]

The distinctive vocal style Jones developed on the trilogy is premised on the way she perceived that 'it would be better . . . to have a voice that suited my appearance' and its associations with masculinity and the crooner.[37] 'When I sing a song I need to get into character,' says Jones of the way she harnesses the voice as body to portray a character with masculine overtones.[38] By way of contrast, where a figure such as Diana Ross would duet with Marvin Gaye on *Diana and Marvin* (1973) to achieve a male/female interplay, on 'Unlimited Capacity for Love', double tracking allows Jones to duet with herself by shifting between the deep voice used for half-speaking and the higher one used for half-singing on the track.

This testing of gender boundaries was prepared by Jones's formative relationship with her brother. 'We easily passed ourselves off as twins and I wonder if we were somehow tangled up inside my mother,' Jones rationalizes: 'I was born a little more masculine, a girl with some of the boyness Chris lacked. Sexuality can be much more fluid.'[39] Jones renders gender boundaries fluid not only with her vocal style and lyrics but in live performances, presenting what she refers to as 'the male part . . . where the audience is waiting and I'm giving'.[40] The fluidity that results from testing gender boundaries extends into Jones's choice of fashion designers, including Giorgio Armani, as she wore the traditional attire of the crooner, the suit, on both the cover of *Nightclubbing* and in the video for 'Pull Up to the Bumper'. Just as important a designer for Jones is Issey

Miyake, whose sculptural garments are visible on the LP cover of *Warm Leatherette* and in numerous concerts of the period, 'the flamboyant costumes and exaggerated gestures' theatricalizing live performances.[41] 'Through [Issey Miyake] I learned about . . . Kabuki [theatre],' says Jones, 'and this was a massive influence on how I would present myself as a performer,' since early kabuki females frequently played male roles.[42] Initially associated with the definition of a conservative form of masculinity, the crooner archetype provides Jones with a framework in which to question it.

Jones's emphasis on flamboyance and the exaggerated as part of a process of questioning gender roles by reworking the crooner archetype is another way of articulating Susan Sontag's 'camp'. 'Camp responds particularly to the markedly attenuated and to the strongly exaggerated,' writes Sontag, '[and] the androgyne is certainly one of the great images of Camp sensibility.'[43] Sontag continues: 'Allied to the Camp taste for the androgynous is something that seems quite different but isn't: a relish for the exaggeration of sexual characteristics and personality mannerisms.'[44] Jones exaggerates the sexuality of her persona through the way each aspect of her appearance is styled in such a high-keyed manner. While a transgender singer such as ANOHNI tests these gender boundaries to an even greater degree today, Jones in 1980 was radical, her performances as a female vocalist having an immediate impact on figures such as Annie Lennox, who coloured Jones's Muhammad Ali flattop orange, wore a crisp white shirt under Jones's Armani suit, and extended her vocal range.

In addition to issues pertaining to gender, Jones's border crossing also addresses assumptions of race through both the multi-racial composition of the Compass Point Allstars and her own personal trajectory. Having arrived in the United States in the early 1960s from Jamaica, Jones felt 'Black, but European. European, but Jamaican,' being constituted from 'a mixture of places and accents that I added to as I moved around, constantly relocating myself physically and mentally.'⁴⁵ This diversity inbuilds a complexity into the Compass Point Trilogy and the retooling of the crooner archetype.

Other singers continued Jones's border crossing by working with the Compass Point Allstars to record albums in Nassau throughout the 1980s – including, among many others, Ian Dury's *Lord Upminster* (1981), Joe Cocker's *Sheffield Steel* (1982) and Gwen Guthrie's *Portrait* (1983) – but the intensity of the Compass Point Trilogy was never repeated. Even Serge Gainsbourg's second LP with members from the group in 1981, recorded at Compass Point, sounds like a diluted version of *Aux armes et cætera* from two years earlier. Following the rise of the record label ZTT, Jones opted to work with Trevor Horn on her next LP, *Slave to the Rhythm* (1985), wisely letting the Compass Point series remain just a trilogy, and looking for moments of dissonance elsewhere. The crooner would continue to develop into the mid-1980s, but its vitality lay elsewhere.

Ian McCulloch of Echo and the Bunnymen, 19 July 1983,
Royal Albert Hall, London.

8

Ian McCulloch: 'Ocean Rain' (1984)

I t is early 1984 in Studios des Dames, Paris, and Ian McCulloch is attempting to lay down the vocals for the title track of Echo and the Bunnymen's LP *Ocean Rain*. The band, consisting of Pete de Freitas on drums, Les Pattinson on bass and Will Sergeant on guitar, successfully recorded the instrumental tracks for the LP while in Paris, but McCulloch was unhappy with the vocal takes, re-recording them back in Liverpool. Fusing the rumble of Jim Morrison's baritone with the histrionics of David Bowie's higher range, McCulloch's voice on *Ocean Rain* is that of the most powerful crooner of the 1980s, which is no small feat, as the decade was full of them: think of Ian Curtis of Joy Division, Peter Murphy of Bauhaus, Dave Gahan of Depeche Mode and Neil Arthur of Blanc-mange. McCulloch was fascinated by Frank Sinatra, 'Even against Leonard Cohen's, Bowie's, or whoever's – Frank Sinatra's is the best voice. My favourite was the period in the 1960s when his voice was just unbelievable.'[1] McCulloch's voice at the climax of 'Ocean Rain' is equally unbelievable.

The only vocalist in this book who was not a solo artist, the Bunnymen are essential to the development of McCulloch as a crooner, and their collective road to developing *Ocean Rain* was a long and involved one. The Bunnymen first tested out all but two of the songs destined for the LP at a Peel Session recorded at the BBC's Maida Vale studio in early June 1983, including 'Silver', 'Seven

Seas', 'The Killing Moon', 'Nocturnal Me', 'Watch Out Below' (an early version of 'The Yo Yo Man'), 'Ocean Rain' and 'My Kingdom'. While both vocally and instrumentally these versions of the songs are incredibly coarse – not benefitting from the simple directness of the Peel Session format as per their previous dates for the BBC between 1979 and 1982 – as part of the Bunnymen's working process, they are crucial. The band titled their triumphant July 1983 concert at the Royal Albert Hall 'Lay Down Thy Raincoat and Groove' – a tongue-in-cheek reference to their dress code as mirrored by their most ardent fans and the electro-pop of their most recent single 'Never Stop' – and aired two of the new tracks, 'The Killing Moon' and 'Silver'. As per the Peel Session, these are taken at quite a clip and sound overtly rough, the electric guitars and the aggressively played string instruments bullying rather than caressing the songs into shape. Better are the versions of two of the songs from the Peel Sessions, 'Silver' and 'The Killing Moon', performed for a TV special commissioned by the BBC titled *Life at Brian's*. More apposite for being purely acoustic, and with carefully played string accompaniment, the treatment is nevertheless still too skiffle-like – that is, rough and played on acoustic guitar – to do justice to the more delicate aspects of the songs. As on both the Peel Session and at the Royal Albert Hall, McCulloch's singing is frequently off pitch – criminal for a crooner.

The Bunnymen rounded out 1983 with a set for Channel 4's *The Tube* consisting of only new material, 'Nocturnal Me', 'Ocean Rain', 'The Killing Moon' and 'Thorn of Crowns' (alternatively titled 'Cucumber'). With de Freitas swapping sticks for brushes, Pattinson and Sergeant alternating between acoustic and electric instruments, and accompanied by a carefully played cello, the band do justice to the new songs, finding their optimum tempo. McCulloch's singing is more controlled, its range and delicacy coming through for the first time. Appropriately, the mood created is much more scenic than anything the band had previously attempted.

Ian McCulloch of Echo and the Bunnymen, 19 July 1983,
Royal Albert Hall, London.

The first track to be recorded for *Ocean Rain* was 'The Killing Moon', cut at Crescent Studios in Bath in December 1983, with McCulloch's vocals laid down at Amazon Studios in Liverpool later in the month, and released as a single in January 1984. Using acoustic twelve string, brushed drums and thrumming upright bass, and cut through with the distant jangle of a wiry, reverb-drenched electric guitar, the double-tracked singing near the end of the track is McCulloch's most impressive to date. Just prior to fading out on both the 12″ and the later released LP version of the song, McCulloch momentarily drops to a lower register while singing the refrain about fate, the deeper voice occupying space beneath the treble strings and guitar as they build. Not as deep as the voice of Barry White, McCulloch's voice on this passage nevertheless gives a nod to White's spoken-word segment on the track 'Bring Back My Yesterday' (1973), its conversational tone seeming to address the listener more directly. Contrasting against the baritone segment as it fades, McCulloch returns to the higher voice used on each previous chorus of 'The Killing Moon'. No other new-wave figure was capable of such controlled crooning.

As with all of *Ocean Rain*, 'The Killing Moon' is harnessed by a return to direct songwriting. 'After *Porcupine,* which was intense and complicated,' says drummer de Freitas, '[we] wrote in our flat in Liverpool . . . with acoustic guitars.'[2] Driving this return to basics was how the band were 'looking for a more melodic thing'.[3] This more direct approach to songwriting returned the Bunnymen to their first LP, *Crocodiles,* but the overtly melodic element was new. On this note, it's no coincidence that on the acoustic set the band produced for the BBC documentary *Life at Brian's* they chose to either showcase new songs from *Ocean Rain,* including 'Silver' and 'Seven Seas', or to return to 'Stars are Stars' and 'Villiers Terrace' from *Crocodiles.* With the possible exception of 'All My Colours', material from the two LPs in between – *Heaven Up Here* (1981) and *Porcupine* (1983) – simply would not have worked acoustically. The acoustic-based, melody driven songs perfectly complement McCulloch's newly extended vocal abilities.

The instrumentation on *Ocean Rain,* which was released in May 1984, complements this direct but more mature approach to songwriting, with Sergeant's lead guitar, Pattinson's bass and de Freitas's drumming all moving up a few notches technically. *Ocean Rain* consolidates the band's use of strings piloted on two of *Porcupine*'s tracks, 'The Back of Love' and 'Heads Will Roll'. Complementing the strings and the use of acoustic guitars on *Ocean Rain* are a wide array of instruments, including a xylophone and glockenspiel played by de Freitas and a harmonium played by Sergeant. Together with the songwriting, the expanded instrumentation on *Ocean Rain* enables the band to 'make something conceptual with lush orchestration', explains Sergeant.[4] This approach to orchestration triggers 'the whole [windswept] mood . . . European pirates . . . dark and stormy, battering rain; all of that'.[5] Side 1 of *Ocean Rain* opens with its fastest song, 'Silver', full of Sergeant's chiming twelve-string guitar and underpinned by de Freitas's tom-tom fills. While the songwriting on the band's previous two LPS may not have impacted the compositions on *Ocean Rain*, the lessons in dynamics that the band learned on *Heaven Up Here* – particularly on the ballads 'All I Want' and 'Turquoise Days' – were put to dramatic use on 'Crystal Days' and 'My Kingdom', as they build from near silence to a deafening wail of clashing guitars and then dramatically return to near silence again. Together with the sound effects explored on *Porcupine* – especially on the LP's title track – the Bunnymen now had an impressive sonic palette to draw from, providing a richly textured backdrop for McCulloch's voice.

Positioned as the final track on Side 2 of the LP, the song 'Ocean Rain' – a torch ballad addressing what is traditionally referred to as a female subject: a ship – begins with Pattinson's acoustic bass, followed by a series of reverb-drenched guitar sound effects captured by studio engineer Henri Loustau. 'They had all these old reverb units, huge things that you just don't get in [most] studios,' says Sergeant of Studios des Dames, which produced a very 'big sound'.[6] The impression of a distant siren during the opening notes of 'Ocean Rain' created by Sergeant's guitar is followed by McCulloch's first line about being at sea again. Gradually, the strings enter. As the track hits the first chorus, de Freitas's brushes start to subtly tease out a beat. The orchestra begins to cushion the spaces around the voice, guitar, bass and drums as the song builds. Suddenly, Sergeant's guitar jumps forward, playing a minimal and repetitive lead line. Then McCulloch re-enters, the vocals coming slightly more forward in Gil Norton's mix before dropping into the deeper Barry White-esque spoken voice with the couplet about the ship's tender frame. Just as 'Ocean Rain' seems to be building into a crescendo with the drums, bass and guitar picking up in both pace and volume, it calms back down again, with an abrupt segue into another verse. McCulloch re-enters, followed by another climactic instrumental break. Now McCulloch wails the line that begins with the word 'screaming' in full voice. What's so appealing about McCulloch's singing on 'Ocean Rain' is the way its power is held back until this late in the song. But instead of closing on this top note – routinely the final one for a crooner – the song ends with a quieter bass note. Sinatra would frequently end a power torch ballad like this, as can be seen in 'Ebb Tide' or 'What's New?' from *Only the Lonely* (1958). To optimize the artifice at their disposal, the crooner has to instinctively know when to emote and when to pull back, as McCulloch does on 'Ocean Rain'.

Vocally, two sources are key to McCulloch: Jim Morrison and David Bowie. The most important Doors LP for McCulloch was arguably *The Soft Parade* (1969). Interestingly, the LP is the least regarded of the Doors albums, with the opening track 'Tell All the People' featuring a heavy orchestral arrangement, the ladled-on strings and brass cradling Morrison's bruised baritone. *The Soft Parade* is usually credited as being too 'soft' – an accusation the band predicted by reflexively factoring it into the LP's title – and not exhibiting either the progressive psychedelic tendencies of their first two releases or the rootsy blues rock of their last two. As rock-driven pop music took hold with the British invasion and then opened out onto LA psychedelic rock in the late 1960s with bands such as the Doors, crooning and critical praise seldom went hand in hand. The ballad 'Indian Summer' from *Morrison Hotel* (1970), the Doors' next LP after *The Soft Parade*, is equal in importance to 'Tell All the People'. Morrison had no doubt heard Sinatra's version of the Victor Herbert torch ballad 'Indian Summer' from the LP cut with Duke Ellington, *Francis A. and Edward K.*, released two years earlier in 1968. Beyond just sharing a title and theme, both songs rise and fall in intensity from verse to chorus and are underpinned with a vocal performance that subtly changes in volume and emotional pitch. Though frequently acknowledging Sinatra as an influence, Morrison's vocal style is actually a composite of the crooner and the blues belter Willie Dixon.[7]

Complementing Morrison's deeper range, McCulloch deploys Bowie-like histrionics when reaching for higher notes on 'Ocean Rain', as per 'Word on a Wing' from *Station to Station*. McCulloch tells of first becoming aware of Bowie when watching a performance of 'Starman' on *Top of the Pops* in July 1972. 'What I loved about Bowie', says McCulloch, '[was] the sound of his voice being from another planet.'[8] McCulloch first experienced Bowie live as the Thin White Duke on the *Station to Station* tour at Wembley in May 1976.[9] Catapulting the songs towards a higher emotional plane, McCulloch first presses Bowie's histrionics into service on *Heaven Up Here* (1981). Unjustly overlooked, the final track on *Heaven Up Here*, the smouldering 'All I Want', finds McCulloch reaching the same emotional heights as Bowie does on 'Word on a Wing'. McCulloch's crooning on 'Ocean Rain' near the climax of the song makes full use of this histrionic technique, first practised on the earlier tracks.

Rather than using more contemporary singers such as Bowie as a touchstone to avoid having recourse to Sinatra, as Grace Jones does in 1980, McCulloch constantly praises the voice Sinatra developed in the 1960s, later choosing to cover 'Summer Wind' from the LP Scott Walker derided on its release: *Strangers in the Night* (1966).[10] Though less vocally flexible in terms of sustaining and bending notes, Sinatra is more stylistically flexible during the 1960s, as demonstrated by the embrace of bossa nova with the first Antônio Carlos Jobim LP. Sinatra's LP with Jobim from 1967 finds arranger Claus Ogerman identifying the most apposite way of weaving the singer's voice and the Brazilian composer's guitar playing and melodies together. Ogerman provides a series of charts that nurture Sinatra's voice just as much as Nelson Riddle's in the 1950s but in a way that sounds contemporary to 1967.[11] Tracking Jobim down by phone at a Rio de Janeiro bar in December 1966, Sinatra made plans with the composer to travel to LA to record *Francis Albert Sinatra and Antônio Carlos Jobim* early the following year. Taking place on three evenings in January 1967, the sessions began, as Warner/Reprise executive

Stan Cornyn reports in the LP's liner notes, 'like the World Soft Championships', with Sinatra commenting, 'I haven't sung so soft since I had the laryngitis,' and the trombonist on the date bemoaning, 'if I blow any softer, it'll hafta come out of the back of my neck.' With its use of brushes, upright bass and acoustic guitar – and both the strings and brass subtly cushioning them – the LP is one of the most gorgeous in Sinatra's back catalogue, ushering the singer's most intimate vocal performances to date. The final track on the LP, 'Once I Loved', is the nearest overall precedent to the Bunnymen's 'Ocean Rain'. Although the song doesn't build in a relatively linear way, as 'Ocean Rain' does, the use of dynamics such as silence and space find multiple points of correspondence between the two, with Ogerman's arranging chair in 1967 being filled by Adam Peters in 1984. It's not difficult to imagine Sinatra singing either 'Ocean Rain' or 'The Killing Moon' accompanied by Jobim.

The Doors' *The Soft Parade* and Bowie's *Station to Station* may be the key LPs vocally for McCulloch in 1984, but they are not the vital ones instrumentally for the Bunnymen. 'The only real likeness I can see is Mac's voice, and I don't even really see that,' commented de Freitas on the comparisons critics made between the two bands, pointing out that 'keyboards featured very strongly with the Doors, but not with us.'[12] More important to the Bunnymen at this point instrumentally is the psychedelia of albums by two other LA-based bands: Love's *Forever Changes* (1967) and the Byrds' *The Notorious Byrd Brothers* (1968). While on the surface the Moody Blues' *Days of Future Passed* (1967) seems to occupy this position because of its orchestral settings, with its insistence on bringing contradictory elements into collision – soft orchestral washes contrasted with stinging garage guitar solos and chiming Rickenbacker riffs – *Ocean Rain* is closer to LA psychedelia. Ranging from deftly crafted three-minute pop songs to extended, open-ended instrumental workouts such as *Forever Changes* and *The Notorious Byrd Brothers*, the Bunnymen's *Ocean Rain* is stylistically varied. While de Freitas allowed the

Morrison vocal reference at a push, McCulloch emphatically denied the psychedelic one, declaring that 'it doesn't mean anything "psychedelic"' in reference to the Bunnymen's sound.[13] McCulloch's denial of psychedelia was nevertheless an oversight since Bunnymen guitarist Sergeant – who was often in disagreement with the singer – frequently mentioned not only Love and the Byrds but the 13th Floor Elevators and the Seeds in interviews of the period. The guitar attack on 'Thorn of Crowns' and 'My Kingdom' and the flanging effect on 'Crystal Days' was lifted directly from Love's 'A House Is Not a Motel' and the Byrds 'Get to You'. Elsewhere on *Ocean Rain*, Sergeant's chiming twelve-string electric Vox guitar rings out on 'Silver' and 'Seven Seas' in a way akin to McGuinn's on *The Notorious Byrd Brothers* track 'Change Is Now'. The daubs of orchestral colour on The Byrd's ballad 'Goin' Back' and Love's 'Alone Again Or' bring the Bunnymen even closer to both bands. The way the instrumental touchstones for *Ocean Rain* contrast with the vocal ones builds a tension into the LP that accounts for its vitality.

Typified by *Ocean Rain*, approaches to the concept LP in 1984 were returning it to the looser stage it enjoyed from the mid-1950s to the mid-1960s, before it was literalized by the albums that the Beatles' *Sgt Pepper's Lonely Hearts Club Band* (1967) triggered such as the Kinks' *Arthur* (1969) and, later, Pink Floyd's *The Wall* (1979). In 1984 rather than concept albums per se, themed LP collections akin to *Moonlight Sinatra* (1966) seemed relevant again. Other LPs released in 1984 also took advantage of this approach, including David Sylvian's moody *Brilliant Trees* (1984), Siouxsie and the Banshees' string-drenched *Hyæna* (1984), Prince's epic *Purple Rain* (1984) and U2's ambient *The Unforgettable Fire* (1984). Looser and more evocative in conception, these LPs provide a heightened sympathetic setting for the vocalist, as *Ocean Rain* does for McCulloch.

McCulloch's voice on 'Ocean Rain' is the summit of a type of crooning intoxicated with its own grandiosity. 'I'm glad I was born with the voice I've got. 'Cos it can sing "All at sea again/ And now your hurricanes/ Have brought down this ocean rain" and it's brilliant – it's believable.'[14] McCulloch was wary of vocal comparisons to Morrison. 'I have this kind of deepish voice and intonation that might be similar to Morrison's,' McCulloch said in 1984, 'but lyrically, it's quite different. He was the back door man, always having his fire lit. He wrote more about the groin. I'm more cerebral,' he concludes.[15] McCulloch describes how the wording for 'Ocean Rain' 'comes not just from my appreciation of the ocean, but it's a song *for* the ocean . . . I suppose it's a bit Wordsworthian; he felt all those elements were actually speaking, and I suppose I do [too].'[16] Using what could be described as ersatz subject-matter as a starting point, McCulloch rescues it from pure sentiment by introducing a number of darker shadings. The lyrics in the second verse of 'Ocean Rain' do, after all, end with a line about black thoughts. In this way, McCulloch motivates the voice as instrument while negating the voice as person or character.

To launch *Ocean Rain*, the Bunnymen curated the one-day festival 'A Crystal Day' on 12 May 1984 in Liverpool. The crooner became a curator for the day. Consisting of a ferry ride across the Mersey, a bike ride around the city and visits to Brian's diner, Victor's barber shop, the Walker Art Gallery and the Anglican Cathedral, 'A Crystal Day' concluded with the Bunnymen's evening concert at St George's Hall. There the band played three distinct sets, each paginated by a performance from the play *The Monkey King Subdues the White Bone Demon* by the Chinese troupe Dancers of the Pagoda of 100 Harmonies – a nod to nearby China Town. 'Each event dripped heavily with ritualistic symbolism,' explains the band's manager, Bill Drummond.[17] Expanding, McCulloch comments on how 'A Crystal Day' 'was about everything we were in our home town. We used the buildings, the architecture, the river, China Town'.[18] The pride in his hometown even caused McCulloch to outline an 'idea to invent a really long saw and saw Liverpool off from the rest of the country one night when no one's watching . . . just float it off to the . . .

Pacific: we should call it Scouse Islands.'[19] With dramatic increases in local unemployment in the early 1980s causing the Conservative government to adopt a policy that forced Liverpool into a state of 'managed decline', Scouse Islands was a pointed idea. The crooner's local pride was fierce.

With the launch of MTV in 1981, the video became a crucial medium for the crooner from Jones's 'Pull Up to the Bumper' (1981) onwards. While 'The Killing Moon' video could have accompanied almost any pop single released that year – including George Michael's 'Careless Whisper' (1984) – and no video was shot for 'Silver', the second single from *Ocean Rain*, the Bunnymen commissioned Anton Corbijn to direct the one for 'Seven Seas', which was released as the final single from the LP. Using a set resembling the stage of an old music hall, the video starts with heavy theatrical curtains parting to reveal a close-up of a map focused on Liverpool with de Freitas standing in front of it reading the *Liverpool Echo*. Enter McCulloch stage right, wearing scuba diver goggles; sporting

English new wave and alternative musician Ian McCulloch, of the group Echo and the Bunnymen, films the music video for 'The Killing Moon', London, 14 November 1983.

a penguin suit, Pattinson is then pushed on, followed by Sergeant dressed as a fish. Corbijn's surreal humour peaks when during the instrumental break, McCulloch appears in drag, with a blonde wig and full make-up. 'When I walked out with the wig and the lipstick on [the others] couldn't believe it,' says McCulloch; 'it was from when I used to like Bowie a lot and there were all them people wearing make-up, and I suppose at the time I thought, "God, I'd love to be able to dye my hair orange and get the lippy on."'[20] Unlike Bowie, McCulloch equivocates, quickly taking the wig off and wiping away the lipstick as the instrumental break finishes and the vocal part of the middle eight of 'Seven Seas' starts. McCulloch could reference those aspects of camp that Bowie piloted in popular music, but only temporarily, feeling the need to quickly reassert a narrower image of masculinity as projected by figures such as Sinatra or Morrison.

McCulloch's singing easily eclipses the vocal achievements of Nick Cave and Ian Curtis in the early 1980s, although this goes against the grain of perceptions of them today. McCulloch's voice and songwriting quickly matured after the Bunnymen's first LP, *Crocodiles* (1980), and was at its optimum for just a few years, enjoying only short-term impact. By contrast, Cave's voice and songwriting took longer to develop but was the more commercially and critically enduring in the long run. Neither of them had a kind word to say about each other at the time, with McCulloch commenting on how Cave, 'the has-been junkie', was 'a fake, [who] can't sing' and Cave reportedly being less than impressed after attending a Bunnymen concert at the Lyceum in London in 1980 with other members of the Birthday Party.[21] Closer to Liverpool, even when considering just the respective releases of the Bunnymen and Joy Division in 1980, Curtis failed to scale the same vocal heights as McCulloch, but the posthumous reputation the Mancunian enjoys – including a major film, *Control* (2007), which documents Joy Division's exploits – continues to overmagnify his accomplishments to this day, death being the quickest route to rock immortality.

Instead of building on *Ocean Rain* later in 1984, the Bunnymen sacked their inventive manager, Drummond, who had always kept the band edgy by urging them to stage events like 'A Crystal Day', and took a year off. 'This year I'll have to make a solo LP – real Scott Walker stuff,' McCulloch opined, instead recording just one single, a solo version of the classic 'September Song', released at the end of 1984.[22] When asked about covering the song in an interview with Jools Holland on *The Tube*, McCulloch deadpanned: 'I thought people would expect me to do a bit of crooning.'[23] Maybe so, but the single's production and orchestral arrangement by Clive Langer and Colin Fairley, respectively, are bland. McCulloch's plans to release three further singles, each with a different arranger, with Benny and Bjorn from ABBA producing, may have fared better had they been realized.[24] By the time the Bunnymen came back together in 1985 to record a new single, the majestic 'Bring on the Dancing Horses' released in October, and tour in support of a best-of LP, *Songs to Learn and Sing* (1985), crucial momentum had been lost. Instead of taking time off to indulge in sentimental solo projects and releasing a best-of LP, the Bunnymen's bête noire, U2, whom McCulloch consistently sniped about to the press, moved boldly ahead. The two bands had always run in parallel: the raw youth of the first LPs, *Crocodile* and *Boy* (both 1980), respectively; leading to the more sombre second LPs, *Heaven Up Here* and *October* (1981); and the ice-capped summit of their third LPs, *Porcupine* and *War* (1983); being softened with their atmospheric fourth LPs *Ocean Rain* and *The Unforgettable Fire* (1984). The fact that U2 appeared at Live Aid in 1985 and the Bunnymen, ever the curmudgeons, were, as Sergeant recalls, 'more than happy to say no' when invited didn't help matters.[25] But while U2 used *The Unforgettable Fire* as a building block in shaping a new sonic landscape that lead to their blockbuster *The Joshua Tree* (1987), the Bunnymen parked the sound shaped on *Ocean Rain* and released a final eponymous LP, the only one in their catalogue at the time without swagger. If the Bunnymen had gone deeper into the sound created on *Ocean*

Rain, or returned to the basic rock sound of *Crocodiles* – as revealed by the demo versions of new songs, including 'My Heart Is Overflowing' and 'New Direction', originally slated to appear on their 1987 LP – things might have been different. Or perhaps if the Bunnymen had opted to collaborate with producers like Daniel Lanois and Brian Eno, as U2 wisely did from *The Unforgettable Fire* onwards, they may have continued their creative trajectory, given that McCulloch's voice was in peak condition in 1987. As it was, the Bunnymen explored none of these options, and never mattered again. The crooner muse went elsewhere: Cave had just started the Bad Seeds and was progressing towards *The Boatman's Call* (1997), releasing a succession of compelling LPs that reworked the métier of the crooner in new and surprising ways. The future was with the junkie crooner.

9

Nick Cave: 'Far from Me' (1997)

The contrast between the dinner jacket and bowtie and shock of back-combed hair sprouting from Nick Cave's head on the cover of *Kicking Against the Pricks* (1986) signals a radical visual refashioning of the crooner archetype as channelled through Sid Vicious's inebriated version of Frank Sinatra's 'My Way' in Julien Temple's infamous *The Great Rock 'n' Roll Swindle* (1980). Musically, the LP gives a glimpse of the role torch ballads will play in Cave's future. When an interviewer wryly commented that 'your songs are more like torch songs now than torched songs,' Cave replies in the affirmative.[1] Consisting entirely of cover versions, *Kicking Against the Pricks* afforded Cave the opportunity to prioritize his vocals without having to worry about songwriting. 'I discovered a quality in my voice that I didn't realize was there,' a quality enhanced by singing 'softly up close to the microphone', says Cave, identifying the precise moment he embraced crooning.[2] The possibility of writing torch ballads opened up, reaching a summit with *The Boatman's Call* (1997), recorded at Sarm West Studios in London, an LP that features Cave's most emotive singing yet.

Crucial to Cave's development as a crooner are the singing of Johnny Cash, the songwriting of Leonard Cohen and the performance style of Elvis Presley in his final years. Cave often refers to the deep impression left on him from watching episodes of *The Johnny Cash Show* (1969–71) prior to his teenage years, describing Cash as

The Great Rock 'n' Roll Swindle (dir. Julien Temple, 1980).

a 'real bad man . . . dressed in black'.[3] From early appearances onwards, Cave almost exclusively dresses in black himself, second-hand suits soon being replaced by bespoke pieces. Cave's second LP, *The Firstborn Is Dead* (1985), included 'Wanted Man', a track written for Cash by Bob Dylan in 1969, and his next LP, *Kicking Against the Pricks*, included the Cash-penned 'The Singer'. Cave found the perfect accompaniment to the styling of the Man in Black in Cash's baritone. 'With the tone of his voice,' explains Cave, 'you're really hearing every word thundering out,' inevitably lending 'a certain gravity to what he sings'.[4] In his autobiography, Cash recalls the day his voice broke and his mother heard his baritone vocal tone, her eyes tearing. From then on, Cash's mother referred to her son's voice as 'the gift'.[5] The singular qualities of 'the gift' are most evident on Cash's only duet with Dylan to be released during his lifetime, 'Girl from the North Country' (1969). Although he admitted only coming to appreciate the breadth of Dylan's output later in life, Cave attested to buying multiple copies of the LP the duet appears on, *Nashville Skyline*.[6] Also reprised on *The Johnny Cash Show* so influential to Cave, 'Girl from the North Country' reveals the specific timbral qualities of Cash's voice and how they are pressed into the service of interpreting a lyric. Following Dylan's reading of the first verse in the treacly tone that is slathered over the entire *Nashville Skyline* LP, the mood of the song alters dramatically as Cash enters with his first line. Immediately the song seems to increase in emotional gravity. The burnished tone of his voice is enhanced by the way he lags just slightly behind the beat in comparison to Dylan's solo verse. The emotional gravity accompanying the thunder of Cash's baritone is crucial to all of Cave's torch ballads, but especially those on *The Boatman's Call*.

More dynamic than Cash's carefully composed concept albums from earlier in the decade, typified by *Bitter Tears: Ballads of the American Indian* (1964), Cash's two prison albums – *Johnny Cash at Folsom Prison* (1968) and *Johnny Cash at San Quentin* (1969) – perfectly animate both his voice and the figure he cut as the Man in Black. Deeply empathizing with the convicts, Cash seems to virtually assume their persona, both physically, by wearing the same clothes as them for one performance, and in the lyrical content of the songs sung. Underscoring this is the way Cash conceived both prison concerts as coherent conceptual entities – not just in the usual way of sequencing and pacing, but in terms of the subject-matter the songs address, including 'Wanted Man', 'Starkville City Jail' and 'Folsom Prison Blues'. Even the tracks that deal with other subjects, such as 'A Boy Named Sue', are made to feel part of a logical whole as Cash's profane patter in between the songs unifies them.

Cave had the opportunity to work with Cash a year prior to the older singer's death in 2002, recording 'I'm So Lonesome I Could Cry' at Cash's house in Nashville. For once, Cave's voice sounds almost sweet, thrown into light relief by Cash's funereal timbre. Cash's producer, Rick Rubin, had requested Cave write a new song for Cash. '[Rubin] asked me to write a song, and ['Nobody's Baby Now'] was the one that I wrote. And after that I thought "I'm not handing that over. I really love that song, and I'm going to do that.'"[7] Instead Cash and Rubin decided to cover an existing Cave track, 'The Mercy Seat', an apt choice given how the themes of confinement and corporal punishment it explores were influenced by Cash's earlier song 'Folsom Prison Blues' (1957). Cave and Cash's duet on 'I'm So Lonesome I Could Cry' cut that day reveals two similar crooning styles, but each at different periods of development age-wise.

If Cave's vocal and persona cues are taken from Cash, then the lyrical ones chiefly derive from Leonard Cohen's LP *Songs of Love and Hate* (1971):

> I'd never heard anything like it . . . It remains one of the seminal albums that completely changed the kind of music I would make. It was really the first record that showed a way where it was possible to take some of the kind of dark, self-lacerating visions we found in much of the European poetry and literature we were reading in those days and apply them to a kind of rock sound. When the Bad Seeds put out our first record we did a version of 'Avalanche' as the first track . . . as a kind of attempt to set the tone.[8]

On hearing this cover version on *From Her to Eternity* (1984), Cohen commented on how Cave 'took [the song] to the limit' and '[made] the song alive'.[9] Typical of Cave's early solo output, while his thrash version of 'Avalanche' ramps up the dynamics of the original to almost grotesque proportions, Cohen's version displays a range of subtle dynamics that Cave would later make use of on the torch ballads that constitute *The Boatman's Call*. At the beginning of Cohen's 'Avalanche', the orchestra momentarily swells before breaking to reveal naked arpeggio guitar accompanying his voice. Lyrically, the song explores the relations between lovers with a new-found baseness. On 'There Is a War' on the follow-up to *Songs of*

Love and Hate, New Skin for the Old Ceremony (1974), Cohen adds black humour into the lyrical cauldron.

For the first of Cohen's albums to be recorded in Nashville, *Songs from a Room* (1968), the singer used the same producer as Cash, his label-mate on Columbia, who in turn followed Dylan's lead of using Bob Johnston as producer on LPs recorded there from the mid-1960s up to *Nashville Skyline* in 1969. Cohen's *Songs from a Room* strips away even more instrumentation than Cash's Johnston-produced prison albums. Central to each of the arrangements is the quality of Cohen's voice, which Johnston achieves by training three microphones on it and routing them through echo plates for reverb.[10] The Cohen LP Cave was so enamoured with, *Songs of Love and Hate*, released three years later in 1971, contains four tracks recorded for *Songs from a Room* in 1968, filling some of the barren spaces left on the earlier LP with orchestral flourishes in a way that accentuates the dark nature of Cohen's voice as it unleashes a stream of barbed lyrics.

Leonard Cohen performs on stage at the Musikhalle on 4 May 1970 in Hamburg, Germany.

Given how both Cash and Cohen are relatively static in concert, it's no surprise that Cave turned elsewhere for performance cues: to Elvis, also recording in Nashville at the turn into the 1970s. Rather than the sharp-cheekboned youth of the 1950s, or even the showbiz performer of the early 1970s, it's the puffy, pilled-up figure of his final years that so captivates Cave. In a post on his *Red Hand Files* blog, Cave details how watching the closing scenes of the documentary *This Is Elvis* in London in 1981 changed his ideas on performance for good:

> In the final minutes of the film, we see Elvis, on stage in Las Vegas . . . stoned and overweight . . . we can see the pure anguish of his performance, the drugged and mortified eyes, the terrible aloneness, the horror of the moment – his vast soul crucified on the cross of his own body as he blunders through the words . . .[11]

In the next scene Elvis dies, and as the world media reports his death,

> We see the motorcade, the weeping crowds, the coffin, and the flowers, as the film returns to the Vegas concert and Elvis sings the eternally beautiful 'All My Trials'. To me it is immeasurably moving, Elvis's head bowed, his extraordinary voice steeped in sorrow – then the band rises, he lifts his head and sings 'The Battle Hymn of the Republic' and Elvis is resurrected, triumphant. It is pure religion and as powerful as anything I have ever seen. The final shot of him, in slow motion, arms outstretched, and angel wings of his silver cape flung wide, shows his exultant ascent into heaven.[12]

Cave takes Elvis's final act as licence to perform in concert as if a preacher amid his congregation. With the early Bad Seeds, this often involved an aggressive tactile confrontation with the audience, but by the late 1980s this gave way to a tendency to cast an almost-hypnotic trance over them, with Cave accentuating the lyrics of a song by weaving in and out of the baying arms of fans pressed at the edge of the stage. Time has only increased Cave's ability to manipulate his body language in order to accentuate his live vocal performances. In addition to the more theatrical cues taken from Elvis, as Cave roams the stage with a hand-held microphone, the intimate passages in which he sits at the piano singing mostly torch ballads also derive from Elvis. The same concert from Elvis's last tour that concludes the *This Is Elvis* documentary includes a rendition of 'Unchained Melody'. Hunched over the piano, face framed in a helmet of blue-black hair, the sweat pouring down over his pale, puffed-out cheeks, Elvis struggles to deliver a graceful performance of the song, and yet somehow still manages to by investing every fibre of his being into his singing and piano playing. Depending on the material performed and its precise sequencing in the set, during a concert Cave constantly switches between roaming the stage and sitting at the piano.

Cave's first solo single was a cover version of Elvis's 'In the Ghetto' (1984). When compared to other crooners', examples of camp are few within his oeuvre, but the video for 'In the Ghetto' provides one. With punk hair sprouting out the top of his head and wearing a spangled tuxedo jacket, the video pilots the aesthetic later used for the cover of *Kicking Against the Pricks*. Wearing heavy eye make-up, Cave mimes badly while standing in front of a tawdry theatre set. Camp is found in the knowing punk attitude of Cave's clothes and make-up, together with the out-of-sync miming. Logically, the 'In the Ghetto' single, his first cover version, was followed by the LP of cover versions, *Kicking Against the Pricks*.

As Cave realized there was something to his voice, the possibility of writing ballads opened up. The first of them was 'Slowly Goes the Night' from *Tender Prey* (1988), followed by 'Lament' from *The Good*

Son (1990). Written while living in São Paulo, 'Slowly Goes the Night' reveals a lyrical directness new to Cave, permitting the exploration of a more nuanced range of emotions – in this case expressing a sense of sadness at an emotion lost and never to be recaptured, a sentiment typical of torch songs. 'When I explained to someone that what I wanted to write about was the memory of things that I thought were lost for me,' says Cave, 'I was told that the Portuguese word for this feeling was "*saudade*",' which is 'not nostalgia but something sadder'.[13] Cave's newfound focus on his vocals presented a further challenge of its own. '"Slowly Goes the Night" was a bit of a problem in a way because it was a piano composition and the thing was so strong melodically it was a nightmare to put a vocal on. The refrain played by the piano was so strong,' Cave continues, 'it was almost an instrumental, in a sense.'[14] Even though he initially struggled to coordinate piano playing and singing, this type of performance was to become central to Cave's torch ballads from hereon in. The song initially intended for Cash, 'Nobody's Baby Now', features a strong central piano riff, typical of a number of the ballads from Cave's next two LPS, *Let Love In* (1994) and *Murder Ballads* (1996).

By the mid-1990s, Cave's voice was a very different instrument to the one featured on *Kicking Against the Pricks* a decade earlier. Set against sparse piano-driven instrumentation, *The Boatman's Call* features Cave's most intimate and emotive vocals to date. At the time, Cave felt unsure about carrying an LP on vocal strength, but this is precisely what was accomplished. Having come to terms 'years ago with the fact that I couldn't sing like Barry White', Cave explains being

> bowed beneath the limitations of my voice . . . But I like it now. I don't know why. Well, I do sing better than I used to, I have more control than I used to. I've accepted the fact that my voice will always sound the same way: morose, melancholy,

lugubrious, plaintive. No matter what I do those feelings will always be there inside my voice.[15]

Facilitating this new vocal strength is Cave's more direct approach to lyrics. '*The Boatman's Call* songs were new in that they were very much tied to experience,' he explained: 'they were really a poetic articulation of what was going on in my life.'[16] Running what Cave described as 'the whole gamut' from 'the beginnings and . . . ends' of love, it's appropriate that the songs on *The Boatman's Call* are equally split between the two emotional extremes.[17]

Instrumentally, *The Boatman's Call* is Cave's sparsest LP to date, with the Bad Seeds adding only the lightest of touches. Besides Cave's own prominent piano and occasional stabs of Hammond organ, Martyn P. Casey's bass underpins all of the tracks but one, Thomas Wydler's drums feature on eight of them, and recent recruit Warren Ellis's violin appears on just five. That's pretty much it. Together with the new economy in song structure and the lyrical directness, the sparse nature of the instrumentation as mixed by Flood helps push Cave's voice to the fore. With only piano and a subtle bass accompaniment, the opening track on Side 1, 'Into My Arms', spotlights the fuller, almost sculptural sound of Cave's voice. Besides being deeper, it also feels more precise, the full expressive potential of every lyric being realized as the song's protagonist addresses his lover's religion, requesting that the interventionist God she believes in direct her into his arms. Each time the title phrase 'Into My Arms' is repeated, a sharp intake of breath is audible, as if every repetition of the phrase is carefully weighted; applied too heavily, this could feel mannered, but Cave gets it just right. Adding further instrumentation of Hammond organ and drums, the second track, 'Lime-Tree Arbour', situates the romantic scenario described by the opening track in a specific place. The next track, 'People Ain't No Good', raises the first note of scepticism on the LP, as the verses narrate an upbeat story of a relationship and the chorus repeats the accusatory title refrain over and over again. 'Brompton Oratory' and 'There Is a Kingdom' follow, and the last song on Side 1, '(Are You) the One That I've Been Waiting For?', returns the narrative to the upbeat nature of the first two songs. While Side 2 kicks off with 'Where Do We Go Now But Nowhere?', pulling on the sceptical note raised earlier, the remaining songs are all positive in nature bar one, the LP's penultimate track, 'Far from Me'.

Underpinned by Casey's bass and Wydler's drums (played using brushes), with Ellis's violin gently scratching in the background, Cave enters on 'Far from Me' with a lyric describing being born to be with the object of his affection and now dying because of her absence. As the piano is introduced, the violin drops out, slightly lifting the next couplet, which describes how he and this woman were lovers in a world where people use one another. Everyone except Wydler then lays out for a bar until the chorus, which repeats the song title 'Far from Me'. The Hammond organ enters on the second verse and runs right through the rest of the track as Cave circles around the subject, until reaching the middle section, which ends on an incredulous note as the protagonist, raising his voice, asks the woman not to come to him with news of her current life. The last words of the middle section find Cave in full voice, contrasting with the variation on the chorus that follows, for which he returns to the intimate vocal style of the rest of the song. Using contrasts in volume for emphasis too frequently leads to them losing their impact, but using them sparingly as Cave does here ensures that they retain their effectiveness. '"Far from Me"', explained Cave, 'documents the slow deterioration of a relationship . . . it starts quite beautifully and ends quite bitterly.'[18]

Implying that *The Boatman's Call* was triggered by the end of his relationship with singer PJ Harvey, Cave in 2019 on *The Red Hand Files* gave a fuller account:

> The record was . . . the compensatory largesse for a broken heart . . . The break up filled me with a lunatic energy that gave

me the courage to write songs about common place human experiences (like broken hearts) openly, boldly and with meaning – a kind of writing that I had, until that date, steered clear of, feeling a need to instead conceal my personal experiences in character-driven stories.[19]

By offering various ways into its subject of love gone wrong, and mixing the upbeat with the downbeat, the emotional picture that the LP paints seldom feels fixed to the specific, offering the listener multiple access points. *The Boatman's Call* remains a singular item in Cave's expansive discography – so singular, in fact, that Cave was

Nick Cave and the Bad Seeds perform at Open'er Festival on 4 July 2018 in Gdynia, Poland.

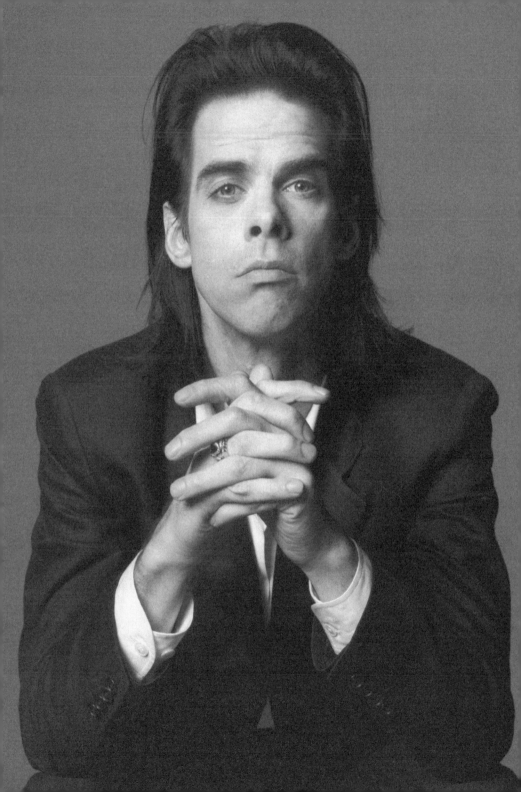

unable to follow the LP with anything, falling silent for four years, the longest gap between albums to date. 'Some records feel like dead ends,' Cave later admitted: '[*The*] *Boatman's Call* was like that. I made it and I just didn't know what to do next. It took a long time to be able to work out where to go after that.'[20] Only a new cycle in his life marked by a new romantic relationship triggered new material, which commenced with *No More Shall We Part* in 2001.

When asked in an interview if he would like to have a voice like Sinatra's, Cave firmly replies in the negative: 'No. That would be jumping out of the frying pan and into the fire. I think trading my voice for Frank Sinatra's would be a pretty poor deal all round. Neither of us would fulfil our potential.'[21] Both the interviewer and Cave probably have in mind the voice of a more youthful Sinatra. If they were familiar with Sinatra's aged voice on 'Long Night' from *She Shot Me Down* (1981), his final LP of torch ballads, Cave's response to the loaded question posed by the interviewer may have been different. As an LP of torch ballads emphasizing the voice, *The Boatman's Call* sits comfortably next to *She Shot Me Down*. There is a weight to the way Sinatra uses his aged voice to interpret torch ballads on *She Shot Me Down* that makes it appropriate when considering Cave's LP. Where Sinatra's viola-like voice on *Only the Lonely* (1958) reveals hurt and bitterness, there is always a sense that the relatively youthful narrator – Sinatra was in his early forties at the time – will endure as time moves on, but the cello-like voice on tracks such as Alec Wilder's 'A Long Night' from *She Shot Me Down* have a finality to them.

Prior to *The Boatman's Call*, Cave exclusively explored the voice as character. In 1988, the year of the LP *Tender Prey*, Cave attests to how he has

> always felt much more comfortable writing in the third person.
> I would find it impossible to write . . . from the author's point

Studio portrait of Australian singer-songwriter Nick Cave during the promotion of his duet with PJ Harvey, 'Henry Lee', from the album *Murder Ballads*, 1995.

Nick Cave in concert in Hamburg, Germany, in July 2001.

of view about myself. But I could write it quite easily by putting a character in to portray me and writing from an outside point of view.[22]

This tendency changes radically with *The Boatman's Call*, when, for the first time, Cave sets accounts of personal experiences in the first person. With this comes a corresponding shift away from exploring the voice as character towards a tendency to establish the voice as person – achieved by Cave's studious transformation of his voice as instrument from *Kicking Against the Pricks* onwards.

By telegraphing the tonal qualities of Cash's voice using Cohen's lyricism, and animating them both with the performance style of Elvis's last years, Cave radically refashions the crooner archetype.

While lacking the vocal virtuosity of either Scott Walker or David Bowie, Cave's facility to combine these disparate qualities on *The Boatman's Call* led the crooner archetype somewhere unexpected. The Anton Corbijn photograph that graces the front cover of *The Boatman's Call* shows Cave wearing a suit jacket, a fitting visual equivalent of Cave's vocal approach on the LP: far moodier than *Kicking Against the Pricks*, with the overt spikiness flattened out to reveal the new intensity afforded by the radically refashioned crooner archetype.

The American rapper Nas and the Jamaican reggae artist Damian Marley released the collaborative album *Distant Relatives* (2010). The former is pictured here at a live concert at Vega in Copenhagen, 6 July 2010.

10

Nas: 'Bye Baby' (2012)

In 2012, the rapper Nas recorded the introspective *Life Is Good* between studios in New York, LA and Miami. The LP includes songs that chart aspects of the demise of a relationship, using language previously considered too coarse for a torch ballad. Imagine how Frank Sinatra really spoke in private about the subject-matter of the torch ballad – replete with slang and expletives – finding its way into song, and you get a sense of the place Nas occupies in the trajectory of the crooner.[1]

Where Sinatra emphasized the singing voice in the 1950s, and Barry White mixed in the spoken voice in the 1970s, from the 1990s onwards Nas exclusively used the spoken voice. The gradual shift in sensibility away from the singing voice and towards the spoken voice introduces a further dynamism into the crooner archetype. Nas goes some way to directly address this issue by firming up his relationship to Sinatra. Tellingly, this begins a year after releasing the torch-ballad-loaded *Life Is Good*, with Nas revealing details of the unreleased track 'Sinatra in the Sands', a play on the title of the live LP *Sinatra at the Sands* (1966). A year later again, and the rapper slips into a tux to stage the twenty-year anniversary of his celebrated debut LP *Illmatic* (1994), performed with the National Symphony Orchestra at the John F. Kennedy Centre for the Performing Arts in Washington. More recently, lyrics for the track 'The Pressure' (2021) find Nas referring to Sinatra as a Rat Pack 'nigga'. Like the disco crooner and the new-wave crooner, the rapper crooner may seem like an oxymoron, but the sonic evidence Nas presents on 'Bye Baby' suggests otherwise.

Crucial to Nas's eventual embrace of the crooner are the vocal innovations piloted by the rapper Rakim in the late 1980s. For Nas, Rakim presented an alternative to the way earlier rappers shouted on the mic.[2] Rakim recalls his own response to the limitations imposed by the vocal attack of these rappers in the early 1980s, explaining how the likes of Run-DMC

> kinda shouted on the mic as if they were giving a pep talk to a football team before the Super Bowl . . . If people were going to really hear my ideas and the intricacies of my rhymes, it was better to have a calmer delivery . . . I liked being more conversational because then I could have more control over the tones in my voice, and you'd be better able to really hear me.[3]

Rakim also attests to the importance of developing an intimate connection with the audience by fashioning a more intimate type of vocal approach, a lesson partly learnt from observing Sinatra:

> Sinatra just felt genuine. He was able to use his voice and put his songs together in such a way that he came across as a regular person who knew how to sing . . . And when I listen to his singing today, there's still that special something about it. Listen to 'Fly Me to the Moon'. When you hear it, you can envision the canvas as Frank was painting it: the band in a smoke-filled room, him on stage, sitting or standing, drink in one hand, cigarette in the other. He was the biggest star at the time, but he made people feel like he was just like them. On a stage, standing casually with a drink and a cigarette talking to the people, he bridged the gap between the performer and the audience.[4]

Rapper Nas performs 'Rock Bells'.

Rakim's debut LP with Eric B, *Paid in Full* (1987), provides a
marked alternative to Run-DMC by developing an approach to rapping that opens up its range to incorporate the more intimate vocal
style essential to any crooner. Tracks such as 'Move the Crowd' and
'Eric B Is President' reveal a more nuanced type of delivery. While
expanding the possibilities of vocal delivery, the content of Rakim's
lyrics do, however, turn on two of the most routine subjects of hip
hop: boasting about one's rapping ability and one's wealth. In 1987,
the emotional intelligence required in order to lyrically broach the
subject-matter of the torch ballad remained distinctly outside the
remit of even the most progressive rapper.

While the use of Rakim's more intimate vocal approach is essential to Nas's development as a crooner, so too is the embrace of more
emotive subjects lyrically. To this end, the lyrics on *Illmatic*, produced by DJ Premier, Q-Tip and Large Professor, reveal a heightened
sense of urban realism, with the rapper formulating compelling
first-person narratives to explore an individual's response to his
environment. The verses of 'One Love', for example, consist of a

series of letters composed by Nas to incarcerated friends, describing events that have taken place following the receivers' imprisonment. Developing a sophisticated form of wordplay, part of the first verse includes lines describing the birth of a son. Gradually moving towards the torch ballad, Nas's exploration of more personal and emotive subjects and use of a more intimate vocal style sounded fresh in hip hop in 1994.

The subject-matter broached by the lyrics on *Illmatic* affect the listener so deeply for being delivered using Nas's distinctive husky vocal timbre, one previously associated with a crooner who often operated in Sinatra's shadow but is actually quite distinct: Tony Bennett. Recorded later in Bennett's career, the LP *Astoria* (1990) is an homage to the singer's place of birth in Queens, with a black-and-white portrait of Bennett from the 1940s standing in front of his childhood home filling the cover. Generations later, Nas employs the same visual cue on *Illmatic* by mapping a facial portrait of himself taken as a child onto a photograph of his childhood home, the Queensbridge housing projects in Queens. Setting *Astoria* and *Illmatic* side-by-side highlights the dramatic shift in sensibility that has taken place between the 1950s and the 1990s. With the exception of 'Boulevard of Broken Dreams', in which Bennett's LP is full of sweet personal odes to Astoria – typified by 'The Folks Who Live on the Hill' and 'A Little Street Where Old Friends Meet' – each of the tracks on Nas's LP, exemplified by 'NY State of Mind' and 'Life's a Bitch', reflects the negative impact of the social changes that have taken place since Bennett's era by emphasizing the economic pressures that lead individuals to crime. The contrast reveals how the contemporary crooner actively confronts rather than just accepts the social conditions of their upbringing. Rap's inherent lyrical profanity is a part of this. In unison with this shift, whereas Bennett's voice only became husky with age, Nas's exhibited this quality from the start. One of the first documented responses, by radio DJ Bobbito Garcia, to the mature quality of Nas's voice highlights the degree to which his voice resonated: 'The motherfucker didn't sound like anybody, like anybody. He had that raspy deep voice for a sixteen-year-old that didn't even make sense. He was young, right? So he had that projection.'[5]

Even though only twenty at the time of *Illmatic*, Nas's 'raspy deep voice' gives an impression of advanced maturity, accentuating the lyrics' exploration of how the harsh urban experiences children are exposed to force them to prematurely reach manhood. Despite this, Nas's voice sounds smooth because of his impeccable flow, as each verse seamlessly transitions into the next. The internal rhymes connecting phrases and the compound rhymes linking sentences act like a soothing balm on Nas's coarse vocal texture.

Nas broadens the emotive potential of a lyric and the texture of his voice by extending the relationship between them on his second LP, *It Was Written* (1996). Using the more commercial sound developed with producer Trackmasters, the LP largely turns away from the harsh realism of *Illmatic*. 'I Gave You Power' is an exception. Finding Nas assuming the character of a gun, the lyrics detail the weapon's reservations regarding its role in street violence. Anthropomorphizing a gun to empathize with its use and abuse allows Nas to treat a routine subject of hip hop in a new way. Detailing the life of a young woman striving to define an alternative role within the confines of her community, 'Black Girl Lost' is the other exception on *It Was Written*. The lyrics to the song's verses detail the protagonist's difficult predicament while the chorus reflects on the subject at one remove with a line about how such a girl is the mother of the earth. Again unusual for a male rapper, the song finds Nas extending his emotional range even further by empathizing with a female subject.

Nas's first attempt at an actual torch ballad is 'Undying Love' from *I Am . . .* (1999), a track which articulates the protagonist's response to betrayal. 'Undying Love' details the story of the protagonist murdering his wife and her lover and eventually himself too. Only a rapper could compose a torch ballad by detailing serial murder.

Nas begins to embrace the emotive subjects associated with the crooner and the torch ballad more directly on his next LP, *God's Son* (2002), with 'Heaven' and 'Dance' both broaching issues triggered by the passing of his mother. *Street's Disciple* (2004) continues this work, addressing Nas's forthcoming marriage to the singer Kelis. The LP also includes vocal innovation on the song 'Sekou Story', with Nas switching from his usual husky voice part way through to inhabit the vocal character of the mother of the main character, in order to communicate her response to the death of her son. Sung using a smoother vocal texture, the line in which she confronts her son's body is chilling. When vocal technique and lyrics work in unison, as on 'Sekou Story', impact is greatly heightened.

A torch ballad dedicated to all the lost friends of his youth, 'Can't Forget about You' from *Hip-Hop Is Dead* (2006), finds Nas and producer will.i.am bringing the past and present of crooning together, interpolating elements of historic crooning with contemporary crooning by sampling the voice of Nat King Cole from the ballad 'Unforgettable' (1959). Using the central instrumental riff from the ballad to drive 'Can't Forget about You', Nas includes a brief sample of Cole's voice to round out the last notes of each chorus, the honeyed baritone of the older crooner contrasting against Nas's husky tone running through each verse. As a coda, 'Can't Forget about You' ends with a longer sample from Cole's 'Unforgettable', as if to clue in the casual listener to the source of the sample.

Containing Nas's most intimate singing, *Life Is Good*, released in July 2012, finds the rapper exploring new territory. 'This is my tenth album,' said Nas, '[and] I wouldn't want to hear someone [who'd been] around for a long time talking about the same thing ... [of] how you came up in the hood and how you had to make it out of the hood.'[6] From the LP cover – Nas, in a rare moment of high camp, wearing a white suit holding the wedding dress belonging to Kelis – to the contents, on *Life Is Good* there's a sense of Nas propelling himself away from the sentimental in order to explore a new subject: the after-effects of the sensual. The first release following the disintegration of the marriage celebrated on *Street's Disciple*, *Life Is Good* finds Nas drawing on Marvin Gaye's *Here, My Dear* (1978) – an LP that contains numerous torch ballads detailing Gaye's divorce – to acquire the narrative tools to address his predicament. 'I thought *Here, My Dear* was brave, beautiful, honest, scary and daring,' said Nas: 'I couldn't imagine what Marvin was going through . . . [and] I couldn't imagine me being in a similar position, years later.'[7] Significantly, Gaye's LP and its version of the torch ballad enabled Nas to accomplish what he refers to as opening up hip hop music 'in a way it probably hadn't been opened up before as far as an artist getting into a personal situation'.[8] Revealing the depth of his interest in Gaye, Nas expounded on the premise of *Here, My Dear*:

> Marvin was married to Berry Gordy's sister [Anna Gordy]. She was older than him and she was sophisticated, she was fly. She had the diamonds, the pearls. She knew how to live and she taught him how to live. She was his love and it ended and he chose to do an album about that when other styles of music were becoming popular at the time. He could have took advantage of the new style of music that was hitting. Instead, what he had to do . . . was give this record to her, the money from the record.[9]

Typified by 'Anna's Song' and 'Is That Enough', Gaye's LP oscillates between poignant reflections on the disintegration of a marriage and bitter comments on its financial ramifications. The song 'Time to Get It Together' includes lyrics confessing Gaye's indulgences in drugs and prostitutes and their negative impact on his marriage. Observing the making of the LP from close-up, Jan Gaye, Marvin Gaye's second wife, further fleshed out its context:

[Marvin] started out the story with a musical creation of his marriage to Anna. Marvin restated his vows and sang of the beautiful optimism that surrounded the couple. But that optimism was short-lived. There was infidelity. There was jealousy. There were breakups and breakdowns. There was tremendous anger . . . In telling the tale of not only his marriage but of the divorce proceedings themselves, he asked Anna, 'Is that enough?'[10]

Across its four sides, the songs on *Here, My Dear* are constantly moving back and forth between the poignancy of the torch ballad and the bitterness of the kiss-off song (a song which celebrates the end of a relationship, piloted by Sinatra and developed by Gaye). Every time a tune on *Here, My Dear* explores feelings of genuine loss or regret, the next one undercuts it. For example, 'When Did You Stop Loving Me, When Did I Stop Loving You' is followed by 'Anger', and a song in which Gaye reflects on the possibilities of future love, 'A Funky Space Reincarnation', is programmed before 'You Can Leave, But It's Going to Cost You', a line allegedly spoken by Anna Gaye.

Crucial for Gaye when conceiving *Here, My Dear* was the way Sinatra negotiated the line between the torch ballad and the kiss-off song across the breadth of his work. Gaye was forthright about the importance of Sinatra in his development, commenting on how his 'dream . . . was to become Frank Sinatra. I loved his phrasing, especially when he was very young and pure.'[11] Sinatra's version of the ultimate kiss-off song, 'Goody Goody' (1962), co-written by Johnny Mercer – author of the ultimate torch ballad 'One for My Baby (and One More for the Road)' – is a celebration of a past love's misery.[12]

Predominately produced by No I.D. and Salaam Remi at 4220 in LA, Instrument Zoo in Miami and Jungle City in New York, Nas's *Life Is Good* negotiates the line dividing the torch ballad and the kiss-off song to the point of exacerbation. Side 1 of *Life Is Good* opens with the track 'No Introduction', which details a litany of events from Nas's childhood onwards, including a line reflecting on the role of the new LP in it in providing closure. 'Loco-Motive' follows, sizing up the craziness of the predicament that famous rappers find themselves in, emphasizing the need to keep developing by namechecking Sinatra again. 'Daughters' considers the complexities of fatherhood, and 'Reach Out' returns to the issues addressed in the opening song, measuring the social and emotional distance Nas has travelled since the days of *Illmatic*. 'World's an Addiction' starts to bring the central matter at hand – the disintegration of a relationship – into crisp focus by analysing the availability of everything from drugs to luxury products to help numb acute emotional pain. 'You Wouldn't Understand' contemplates the inability of someone to comprehend the impact a partner's background has on his current life. The verses

Nas performing live on stage in Hamburg, Germany, in 2003.

find Nas again outlining events from his upbringing, and the chorus reflects on receiving a less-than-empathetic response to these experiences. 'Back When' and 'The Don' both revisit the early days of Nas's success. Meanwhile, 'Stay' and 'Cherry Wine' return to the central issue, turning on an admission of emotional need.

By far the boldest song to oscillate between the torch ballad and the kiss-off song on *Life Is Good* – and one Nas highlighted as 'the most important record on the album' – is the final track on Side 2, 'Bye Baby', co-written by Nas with Drake's frequent collaborator, Noah '40' Shebib, and Remi, co-producer of the entire LP.[13] For openers, Nas's husky voice cuts across a smooth vocal refrain by a female backing singer, either Kaye Fox or Hannah Sidibe, starting with lyrics describing a partner who left. As the verse continues, including a lyric about attending counselling together, what sounds like an electronic keyboard played by Shebib gradually comes forward in the mix. Another line addresses the extramarital affairs that Nas's partner's father engaged in, and the impact that they had on her. The female vocal refrain from the intro repeats and then boom-bap drums enter to propel the song forward. The chorus consists of Nas's voice, treated with echo, repeating the song's title phrase over the top of not only the female backing voice but another male voice – Aaron Hall sampled from 'Goodbye Love' – buried deeper in the mix. The drums cease and the second verse begins, the lyrical focus shifting to the past when the pair were happy, the female vocalist recounting support she gave Nas in the face of racist Miami police. The second chorus is followed by the third and final verse, and ends with a lyric about how Nas hopes to remarry in the future. A final chorus, and the song is through.

Nas's constant shifting between the torch ballad and the kiss-off song recalls the way Sinatra and Gaye also traversed the two – except that where Sinatra gives each type its own LP, and Gaye moves between them in the course of a single album, Nas traffics all the way from torch ballad to kiss-off song within one single track. Underpinned by the shift from digital to analogue recording, between the 1950s and the early 2010s there's a sense of time being compressed: where once the expanse of an entire career was needed, and then an LP, today a single track suffices in order to explore the territory between the torch ballad and the kiss-off song. The benefit of this shift is the way feelings such as emotional confusion can be economically conveyed with accuracy. But the spite of the kiss-off song acts as a barrier to the deeper, more sustained emotional exploration of pathos that the torch ballad affords, which is certainly a distinct drawback.

The status of the spoken word in Sinatra's recordings is crucial to an understanding of Nas's development of the crooner archetype. As Johnny Mercer and Cole Porter exclusively used romantic, never profane, language, none of this finds its way into Sinatra's recordings. Informally, every expletive and slang term in Sinatra's speech has been reliably captured by the investigative journalist Pete Hamill, so we have a sense of how the singer actually spoke.[14] Formally, the spoken word plays an important role on three of Sinatra's LPs in the mid- to late 1960s, with extensive spoken-word segments being commissioned for each of them: *A Man and His Music* (1965), *Sinatra at the Sands* (1966) and *A Man Alone* (1969). On *Sinatra at the Sands*, the archetypical crooner, known for his singing voice, commits more than 15 minutes of time to his spoken voice. Sinatra could easily have omitted the spoken sequences from the live LP – Nat King Cole did on an LP recorded at the same venue – but he chose instead to include them. Later accentuated by Tom Waits on the LP *Nighthawks at the Diner* (1975), the spoken voice enters the crooner's arsenal of vocal techniques through the back door provided by live performance. There is a sense here of Sinatra gesturing towards the role that the spoken voice is set to play for the crooner in the future without actually arriving at it. Decades later, Nas does precisely this.

Crucial to Nas's retooling of the crooner is his approach to songwriting. Asked in an interview 'what is your process of [song] writing?', Nas explained: 'I tape other people's songs . . . and I build off them.'[15] Expanding, Nas described how 'I used to tape off the radio . . . [and then] play it the next day, all day, then for a whole month straight. After the month was up, I'd . . . write a whole bunch of songs.'[16] Expedited by the shift from analogue to digital, hip hop's use of the sample pushes Bryan Ferry's treatment of existing songs as readymades in the 1970s one step further, by taking an actual element from an existing track and literally reusing it. The other key development is that where from Scott Walker to Nick Cave the crooners output is optimized when they compose each element of a song – including the chords, melody and lyrics – Nas writes the lyrics and determines their flow, but the instrumentation to which they are set is, in contrast to Barry White in the seventies, provided by the producer, who usually has myriad beats and samples in hand when beginning to work on an LP. Left free to concentrate on lyrics by the changes to the songwriting process heralded by the pioneers of classic hip hop, Nas advances a series of elaborate narrative tools, including using snippets of conversation, as explored on 'One Love', and warping the role of time by telling the story of a shooting in reverse, as per 'Rewind' (2001). With melody subdued, the precise words used in the lyrics become all the more important, surely accounting for why Nas 'fell in love with words' early on.[17] 'I used to keep a dictionary and work with it and then I realized there are more words that exist in the English language than there are in this dictionary,' said Nas, 'so that means you have to buy multiple dictionaries.'[18] Nas's urban dictionary complements these official dictionaries, leading to a more brutal type of torch ballad, rife with profanity. The fundamental songwriters' tool of experimenting with narrative and temporality, and the careful weighting of words, sentences and rhymes, is effectively mobilized by Nas on 'Bye Baby'.

The rappers' development of the tools of the songwriter are optimized because of the way Nas conceives of his voice as an instrument. Growing up with a trumpet-playing father informed Nas's desire 'to sound like an instrument'.[19] Common among crooners, this desire to sound like a horn runs right the way through their history. 'One night I was listening to a record by Lester Young, the horn player,' recalls Gaye prior to recording the vocals for *Here, My Dear*, 'and it came to me. Relax, just relax.'[20] The tendency runs in the other direction too, as horn players are influenced by crooners, with Miles Davis insisting on having 'learned a lot about phrasing . . . when listening to the way Frank [Sinatra]' and 'Nat "King" Cole . . . phrased'.[21] Nas mobilizes his voice as instrument to explore the voice as character by not just narrating the stories presented in the lyrics of different characters, as with 'One Love', or assuming the perspective of an object, as with the gun in 'I Gave You Power', but by actually adopting another person's vocal personality to assume his character, as per the mother in 'Sekou Story'. As Nas has developed myriad vocal approaches, more nuances in his voice have been revealed, and the barbed nature of his youthful husky tone is rounded out.

Nas is acutely aware of the machinations of the concept LP and its role in providing a context for the torch ballad and the voice of the crooner. 'When you get a chance to put a whole LP together with a format,' said Nas, '[the listener] isn't gonna want to sit down and listen to some ill shit all day'; he wants 'to get some type of mental gain. Like reading a book'.[22] Even taking Public Enemy's *It Takes a Nation of Millions to Hold Us Back* (1988) into account, *Illmatic* was arguably the first fully realized concept LP in hip hop, and listening to it is precisely like reading a mash-up of the novels *Last Exit to Brooklyn* (1964) and *Pimp: The Story of My Life* (1967). Nearly two decades later, Nas's *Life Is Good* extended this by focusing on a single relationship. In so doing, *Life Is Good* betrays the influence of two hip hop LPs cut in the two decades since *Illmatic* was released: Kanye West's *808s and Heartbreak* (2008) and Drake's *Take Care* (2011), both albums premised on the torch ballad. These albums significantly impacted the way Nas conceived of *Life Is Good*, providing an example of how a hip hop LP can be devoted to the exploration of a single relationship from multiple perspectives.

As Nas's emotional intelligence increased, the routine macho persona – and its accompanying suppression of camp – so central to the golden-era hip hop of the late 1980s and early 1990s is rendered more complex, though not completely eroded. Where in Sinatra's time machismo was a socially accepted norm, by Nas's it was thoroughly under attack – certainly so by the time of *Life Is Good* in 2012. Attempts by contemporary figures such as Drake to rethink and open out masculinity continue to impact Nas, most noticeably on the recent track 'Replace Me', from *King's Disease* (2020). The rapper crooner prefigured by Sinatra in his torch ballads and experiments with the spoken word, and fully realized by Nas's rapping and use of guest singers and samples on 'Bye Baby', persists with Drake today. The distance Nas traversed from *Illmatic* to *Life Is Good* easily remains the furthest travelled by any vocalist in his retooling of the crooner archetype, producing the most unexpected – and hard-won – reading of the crooner yet.

Conclusion

Each specific figure explored in the chapters of *Crooner* pursued a fresh and entirely unexpected way to retool the three essential categories that the crooner archetype incorporates – the voice, the torch ballad and the concept album. The stylistic differences between Scott Walker in pop, Barry White in disco, David Bowie, Bryan Ferry and Tom Waits in rock, Grace Jones in reggae, Ian McCulloch and Nick Cave in indie rock and Nas in hip hop could not be more pronounced. All of them developed an aspect of the voice as instrument, body, person or character, harnessing it through the writing of a new kind of torch ballad that is set within a contemporary version of the concept LP. With frequent recourse to camp, and emphasizing different degrees of either pathos or bathos, each crooner explores the gamut of emotions between the sentimental and the sensual. In pursuing this over successive generations, the archetype changed stylistically and the creative remit of the crooner was broadened. Walker was the first crooner who not only sang but wrote songs; White was the first to add the role of the producer; and Bowie was the first to encompass all of these roles while also arranging. From Sinatra's Reprise Records and White's Unlimited Gold record label all the way to Nas's Mass Appeal platform, self-determination by institution-building is often a key part of the crooner's modus operandi.

From Walker to Nas, crooners initially stake out new territory with their most forward-looking LPs, including Bowie's *The Rise and Fall of Ziggy Stardust and the Spiders from Mars* (1972), Ferry's shaping of Roxy Music's *Re-make/Re-model* (1972), Waits's *Small Change* (1976), Jones's *Warm Leatherette*, McCulloch's role in Echo and the Bunnymen's *Heaven Up Here* (1981), Cave's *From Her to Eternity* (1984) and Nas's *Illmatic* (1994). Soon after recording this ground-breaking LP, a backward glance is then cast to the traditional crooner. When this is done too literally, by relying on standard songs associated with earlier crooners, the results are usually tepid. Walker's 'The Song Is You' (1969), Bowie's 'Wild Is the Wind' (1976), Ferry's 'These Foolish Things' (1973), Jones's 'La Vie en rose' (1977), McCulloch's 'September Song' (1984) and Cave's 'By the Time I Get to Phoenix' (1986) all add little to earlier interpretations. By contrast, when this backward glance at the crooner is incorporated with their most forward-looking music – fusing the past and the present together – the results can be enthralling. To wit, Walker's 'It's Raining Today' (1969) channels the vocal control specific to earlier crooners but with an entirely different approach to lyrics; White's 'Bring Back My Yesterday' (1973) retains the sentiment of the traditional torch ballad but delivers it using a bass-baritone voice that emphasizes the spoken word; Bowie's 'Word on a Wing' (1976) uses the fullness of voice associated with past crooners but applies it to a contemporary lyric and arrangement; Ferry's 'When She Walks (in the Room)' (1978) taps into the emotional delicacy of past crooners via a more contemporary sound; Waits's 'Ruby's Arms' (1980) harnesses the sentiment common to traditional torch ballads but uses it to push the voice to an extreme; Jones's 'Unlimited Capacity For Love' (1982) extends the compassion of the traditional torch ballad by enhancing its performance through a vocoder; McCulloch's voice on Echo and the Bunnymen's 'Ocean Rain' (1984) recreates the romantic atmosphere crooners conjured in the 1950s to generate a newly majestic sound; Cave's 'Far from Me' (1997) takes the essential element of the torch ballad and strips it right back to the bone; and Nas's 'Bye Baby' (2012) fully developed the spoken-word element piloted by earlier crooners. The tendency to simultaneously look forward while looking back drives a tension into the very kernel of the crooner, and without it, key moments in popular vocal music, including *Scott 3*, *Station to Station*, *Ocean Rain* and *The Boatman's Call*, may never have occured. This accounts for why each crooner's vocal performance on the song that the chapters of this book focuses on is compelling enough to warrant repeated listening.

Each figure to extend the crooner archetype has been clear about the debt they owe to Sinatra. Walker comments on wanting 'to be able to put that styling into a song [as] Sinatra does'.[1] While White never publicly commented on Sinatra, Marvin Gaye, his guiding influence, did: 'I loved [Sinatra's] phrasing.'[2] On finding they were recording at the same studio, Bowie commented, 'Oh my God, Sinatra's here.'[3] Ferry acknowledged how '[Sinatra] has an immaculateness which I admire.'[4] Waits recalled 'listening to Sinatra when I was starting out'.[5] Jones described her conceiving of 'Iggy Pop as the new Frank Sinatra'.[6] McCulloch claimed 'Frank Sinatra's is the best voice.'[7] Cave felt it important to comment: 'I think trading my voice for Frank Sinatra's would be a pretty poor deal all round. Neither of us would fulfil our potential.'[8] Nas not only namechecks Sinatra multiple times in his lyrics but his key vocal touchstone in hip hop, Rakim, attested to how 'Sinatra just felt genuine.'[9] For such a diverse range of innovative musicians to be so engaged with the same figure from the past is highly unusual, and speaks volumes about the centrality of Sinatra to contemporary popular vocal music.

To progressively extend the archetype of the crooner, each vocalist fixed Sinatra's music to his so-called classic period, spanning the years between the mid-1950s and the early 1960s. From Walker through to Nas, whenever they referred to Sinatra it was almost without exception the Sinatra from the Capitol Records period. While extending the crooner archetype in his/her own singing and songwriting, each vocalist's version of the origins of that archetype remains static. Vocalists lose interest in the blueprint as contemporaneous advances in music began to impact Sinatra from the mid-1960s onwards. This means that Sinatra's embrace of the musical styles that dominated popular music post-1964 – from folk rock, bossa nova, the concept LP, soft rock, disco and funk – and up to the 1980s largely goes unnoticed. In some cases, this is justified, because by the mid-1960s Sinatra was innovating only occasionally and mostly lagging behind, as can be seen in his attempts at disco and soft rock. But sometimes this is an oversight, as Sinatra's embrace of R&B, bossa nova and the overt concept LP in the late 1960s is truly engaging and deserves more attention. Not only is the crooner archetype in parallax, but so too is its historical touchstone: Sinatra. In this sense, the optic of the present redefines Sinatra's corpus by bringing different moments of his output into focus. Tellingly, these crooners are not alone in their tendency to reduce Sinatra's output to his Capitol Records period, with leading Sinatra historians also limiting their focus to it and having very little interesting to say about his post-1967 output on Reprise.[10]

In terms of genres of music, the crooner archetype develops from its start in swing with Sinatra to pop with Walker; disco with White; rock with Bowie, Ferry and Waits; reggae with Jones; indie with McCulloch and Cave; and hip hop with Nas. No other archetype has been as persistent as the crooner in the past sixty years, and no other archetype has been so continually overlooked by music historians. In this sense, it's time for the broader historiography of popular music to be rewritten to factor in the crooner. To date, the only writer to acknowledge the ongoing role of the crooner archetype in principle is Simon Frith in *Performing Rites: Evaluating Popular Music* (1996), and in practice, Simon Reynolds in *Rip It Up and Start Again: Post-Punk: 1978–1984* (2005).[11] Other influential music writers – from Greil Marcus to Alex Ross and from Ian Macdonald to Alexis Petridis – all equally overlook its role. Given the persistence of the archetype of the crooner, tracing its myriad ongoing implications is crucial to any future accounts of popular vocal music.

To encourage this fresh account of popular vocal music, new tracks are vital. Using the method piloted by the innovative producer Amerigo Gazaway, a version of Sinatra singing each of the songs featured in this book, from Walker's 'It's Raining Today' to Nas's 'Bye Baby', would make for fascinating listening. On *Yasiin Gaye* (2014), Gazaway presented an imaginary collaboration between Yasiin Bey (a.k.a. the rapper Mos Def) and Marvin Gaye, producing a mashup between the two by mining Gaye's original vocal multi-tracks to build samples to produce new arrangements. Gazaway's new LP of Sinatra singing would be titled *Far from Me*, after Cave's song, to acknowledge the expansive ground being traversed from 1969 to 2012. Opening Side 1, Sinatra's version of 'It's Raining Today' would use the viola-like voice developed on *A Man Alone* (1969) to accompany Wally Stott's orchestration for strings and guitar. To follow, using Gene Page's arrangement, Sinatra's version of White's 'Bring Back My Yesterday' would isolate Sinatra's spoken-word voice as featured on the *A Man Alone* LP and the singing voice from 'Wave' (1969) to cover both vocal aspects of White's track. Using Bowie's arrangement, 'Word on a Wing' would be delivered using Sinatra's emotive but controlled voice, as featured on 'Ebb Tide' (1958). The final track on Side 1, 'When She Walks (in the Room)', would be performed using Ferry's arrangement with Sinatra's voice lifted from the track 'Forget to Remember' (1969).

Kicking off Side 2 of the LP would be Waits's 'Ruby's Arms', sung by the Sinatra of 'A Cottage for Sale' (1959) to Bob Alcivar's arrangement. Next, against the jam by the Compass Point Allstars, Sinatra's version of Jones's 'Unlimited Capacity for Love' would be sung using the voice from the funk-influenced pop of 'LA Is My Lady' (1984). Echo and the Bunnymen's arrangement for 'Ocean Rain', sung softly using Sinatra's voice as featured on 'Once I Loved' (1967), would follow. The LP's title track, Cave's 'Far from Me', sung using the bare arrangement of the original and featuring Sinatra's aged, cello-like voice developed on 'Long Night' (1982), would be sequenced next. The final track on Side 2 would feature Noah '40' Shebib's arrangement for Nas's 'Bye Baby', sung using Sinatra's spoken-word voice peppering the live LP *Sinatra at the Sands* (1966).

While it may never be realized, *Far from Me* puts the theory of the crooner into practice. Featuring Sinatra in his multifarious voices, singing the songs written by successive stages of crooners, would surely generate a richer understanding of the historic development of the crooner archetype while also usefully contextualizing the music of new vocalists typified by Kojey Radical and Alex Cameron as they arrive. As long as catharsis is needed from the fall-out from romantic love, the role of the crooner as our emotional ventriloquist is set to continue.

References

Introduction

1 Allison McCracken, *Real Men Don't Sing: Crooning in American Culture* (Durham, NC, 2015), p. 16. For another fairly contemporary account of the historical role of the crooner, see Lenny Kaye, *You Call It Madness: The Sensuous Song of the Croon* (New York, 2004).

2 McCracken, *Real Men Don't Sing*, p. 16.

3 Bonz Malone, 'O.G.: Frank Sinatra Didn't Take Orders; He Took Over', *Vibe* (September 1995), pp. 106–10.

4 One of the few alternatives is Stephen Holden, 'Guide to Middle Age', *The Atlantic* (January 1984), pp. 84–7.

5 Barry Miles, *Paul McCartney: Many Years from Now* (London, 1997), p. 183.

6 Bob Dylan, *Chronicles: Volume One* (London, 2004), p. 27.

7 Simon Frith, *Performing Rites: On the Value of Popular Music* (Chicago, IL, 1996), p. 187.

8 Ibid., pp. 196–7.

9 Ibid., pp. 198–9.

10 Charles Keil and Steven Feld, 'Commodified Grooves', in *Music Grooves: Essays and Dialogues* (Chicago, IL, 1994), p. 324.

11 See Florian Heesch, 'Voicing the Technological Body: Some Musicological Reflections on Combinations of Voice and Technology in Popular Music', *Journal for Religion, Film and Media*, II/1 (May 2016), pp. 46–9.

12 Tracey Thorn, 'Me and My Microphone', in *Naked at the Albert Hall: The Inside Story of Singing* (London, 2015), p. 181.

1 Frank Sinatra : 'What's New?' (1958)

1 Charles L. Granata, *Sessions with Sinatra: Frank Sinatra and the Art of Recording* (Chicago, IL, 2004), p. 142.

2 Will Friedwald, 'With Nelson Riddle, 1953–1979', in *Sinatra! The Song Is You* (New York, 1995), pp. 237–8.

3 Robin Douglas-Home, *Sinatra* (London, 1962), p. 36.

4 Ibid., pp. 36–7.

5 James Kaplan, *Sinatra: The Chairman* (London, 2015), p. 105.

6 Ralph Gleason, *Celebrating The Duke: And Louis, Bessie, Billie, Bird, Carmen, Miles, Dizzy and Other Heroes* (New York, 1975), p. 78.

7 Donald Clarke, *Wishing on the Moon: The Life and Times of Billie Holiday* (London, 1997), p. 226.

8 Granata, *Sessions with Sinatra*, p. 98.

9 Miles Davis also commented: 'If I could put together exactly the kind of band I wanted, Frank Sinatra would be the singer. Really, my man is Frank Sinatra.' Kaplan, *Sinatra: The Chairman*, p. 484.

10 Sammy Davis Jr, *Why Me? The Autobiography of Sammy Davis Jr* (London, 1989), p. 34.

11 Douglas-Home, *Sinatra*, p. 35.

12 Ibid., p. 34.

13 Kaplan, *Sinatra: The Chairman*, p. 5.

14 Ibid., p. 505.

15 Tracey Thorn, 'A Window Pane', in *Naked at the Albert Hall: The Inside Story of Singing* (London, 2015), pp. 82–3.

16 See John Gill, 'And His Mother Called Him Bill', in *Queer Noises: Male and Female Homosexuality in Twentieth-Century Music* (Minneapolis, MN, 1995), pp. 47–57.

17 Susan Sontag, 'Notes on Camp' [1964], in *Notes on Camp* (London, 2018), p. 9.

18 Kaplan, *Sinatra: The Chairman*, pp. 344–5 and 354–5.

19 Ibid., pp. 357–8.

20 Ibid., p. 790.

21 The only other occasion in which Sinatra uses the spoken voice on a studio LP is with the retrospective *A Man and His Music* (1965), in which narrative segments linking the songs catalogue his life and career. Each of these segments is shot through with vernacular slang. 'All or Nothing at All' is sequenced just before the following spoken segment: '1940 and break number two. I was now a singing employee of Tommy Dorsey, the General Motors of the band business. And man, the loot was out of this world! Every single week another one hundred and twenty-five clams.' Released a year later, *Sinatra at the Sands* (1966) features ribald jokes and interplay with the Vegas audience. During the eleven-minute monologue break, Sinatra recounts the following story: 'My father was called

into school by the principal . . . and he said to my dad, "Here's the diploma, now get him out." That's what he do say. "Get him out."' Concluding the story with a joke about his advancing age, Sinatra breaks into 'You Make Me Feel So Young'.

22 Bonz Malone, 'O. G.: Frank Sinatra Didn't Take Orders; He Took Over', *Vibe* (September 1995), p. 108.

2 Scott Walker: 'It's Raining Today' (1969)

1 Anthony Reynolds, *The Impossible Dream: The Story of Scott Walker and the Walker Brothers* (London, 2009), p. 270.

2 Jeremy Reed, *Another Tear Falls: A Study of Scott Walker* (London, 1998), p. 27.

3 Reynolds, *The Impossible Dream*, p. 80.

4 Ibid.

5 Ibid., p. 86.

6 Reed, *Another Tear Falls*, p. 67.

7 Reynolds, *The Impossible Dream*, p. 135.

8 Keith Altham, 'Scott Walker Hits Out Again', *New Musical Express*, 1 July 1966.

9 Ibid.

10 Reynolds, *The Impossible Dream*, p. 245.

11 Karl Dallas, 'Brel, the Man Who Wrote the Hard-to-Get Rule Book', *Melody Maker*, 26 November 1966.

12 Reynolds, *The Impossible Dream*, p. 176.

13 Ibid., p. 176. The Walker Brothers covered Bob Dylan's 'Love Minus Zero' on their first LP, *Take It Easy with the Walker Brothers* (1965).

14 Ibid., p. 177.

15 Susan Sontag, 'Notes on Camp' [1964], in *Notes on Camp* (London, 2018), p. 24.

16 Ibid., p. 27.

17 See the interview with David Bowie in Stephen Kijak, dir., *Scott Walker: 30th Century Man* (2006). Bowie also produced the documentary.

18 Marc Almond first came to Walker through the collection *Fire Escape in the Sky: The God-Like Genius of Scott Walker*, compiled by Julian Cope for Zoo Records in 1981.

19 Gordon Coxhill, 'Scott Talks about Scott', *New Musical Express*, 22 March 1969, p. 11.

20 Ibid.

21 Nick Jones, 'The Walker Brothers: Walker Plans', *Melody Maker*, 13 May 1967, p. 1.

22 Ibid.

23 Rob Young, *No Regrets: Writings on Scott Walker* (London, 2012), p. 65.

24 Reynolds, *The Impossible Dream*, p. 234.

25 Ibid., p. 173.

26 Ibid., p. 145.

27 Ibid., p. 173.

28 Jones, 'The Walker Brothers', p. 45.

29 Reynolds, *The Impossible Dream*, p. 152.

30 Ibid., p. 216.

31 Ibid., pp. 232–3.

32 Ibid., p. 234.

33 Ibid., p. 235.

34 Scott Walker interviewed in Kijak, dir., *Scott Walker: 30th Century Man*.

35 Michele Monro, *Matt Monro: The Singer's Singer* (London, 2011), p. 154.

36 Reed, *Another Tear Falls*, p. 9.

37 Reynolds, *The Impossible Dream*, pp. 277–8.

38 Reed, *Another Tear Falls*, p. 72.

39 Ibid., p. 34.

3 Barry White: 'Bring Back My Yesterday' (1973)

1 Produced by Joey Reynolds, 1977, Creative Director, 20th Century Fox. See 'Barry White Producing "It's Ecstasy When You Lay Down Next to Me" (1977)', www.youtube.com.

2 See Suzanne E. Smith, *Dancing in the Street: Motown and the Cultural Politics of Detroit* (Cambridge, MA, 1999).

3 Surprisingly, even more important to Gaye than Charles was Sinatra. 'My dream', said Gaye, 'was to become Frank Sinatra. I loved his phrasing, especially when he was very young and pure. He grew into a fabulous jazz singer and I used to fantasize about having a lifestyle like his . . . Every woman in America wanted to go to bed with Frank Sinatra. He was the king I longed to be . . . He was the heavyweight champ, the absolute.' David Ritz, *Divided Soul: The Life of Marvin Gaye* (Boston, MA, 1991), p. 29.

4 White also commented directly on Charles: '[Charles] can cry on record, he can sound humble, or sigh, he can do so much as he sings you his story.' Barry White, *Love Unlimited: Insights on Life and Love* (New York, 1999), p. 175.

5 Robert Gordon, *Respect Yourself: Stax Records and the Soul Explosion* (London, 2013), p. 225.

6 Ibid., p. 237.
7 Tom Rubython, *White Music: The Barry White Story* (Cogenhoe, 2017), p. 227.
8 White, *Love Unlimited*, p. 142.
9 Gaye's biographer, David Ritz, details the importance of Hayes's LP for Gaye in *Divided Soul*, p. 147.
10 White, *Love Unlimited*, p. 99.
11 Ibid., p. 6.
12 Ibid., p. 108.
13 Rubython, *White Music*, p. 197.
14 Ibid., p. 225.
15 Ibid., p. 201.
16 Ibid., p. 196.
17 Ibid.
18 Ibid., pp. 197–8.
19 Ibid.
20 Ibid., pp. 199–200.
21 John Abbey, 'Barry White: The Message Really Is Love', *Blues and Soul* (August 1979), p. 5.
22 Ritz, *Divided Soul*, pp. 212–13.
23 Ibid., p. 212.
24 Jan Gaye, *After the Dance: My Life with Marvin Gaye* (New York, 2013), p. 52.
25 Ritz, *Divided Soul*, p. 181.
26 Ibid., p. 219.
27 Ibid.
28 Richard Dyer, 'In Defence of Disco', in *On Record: Rock, Pop, and the Written Word* (London, 1990), p. 414.
29 Ibid.
30 White, *Love Unlimited*, p. 143.
31 Ibid., p. 142.
32 Ritz, *Divided Soul*, p. 319.
33 Ibid., p. 320.
34 See Russell A. Potter, 'Soul into Hip-Hop', in *The Cambridge Companion to Pop and Rock*, ed. Simon Frith, Will Straw and John Street (Cambridge, 2001), pp. 143–57.

4 David Bowie: 'Word on a Wing' (1976)

1 Dylan Jones, *David Bowie: A Life* (London, 2017), p. 233.
2 Susan Sontag, 'Notes on Camp' [1964], in *Notes on Camp* (London, 2018), pp. 8–9.

3 Cameron Crowe, 'The Playboy Interview with David Bowie', *Playboy* (September 1976).
4 Sean Egan, *Bowie on Bowie: Interviews and Encounters with David Bowie* (London, 2015), p. 93.
5 Ibid.
6 Ibid., p. 376.
7 Ibid., p. 82.
8 Jones, *David Bowie*, p. 225.
9 Alan Light, 'How David Bowie Brought Thin White Duke to Life on *Station to Station*', *Rolling Stone*, www.rollingstone.com, 23 January 2017.
10 Ibid.
11 Ibid.
12 Jones, *David Bowie*, p. 230.
13 Light, 'How David Bowie Brought the Thin White Duke to Life'.
14 Cameron Crowe, 'David Bowie: *Station to Station*', The Uncool: The Official Website for Everything Cameron Crowe, www. theuncool.com, 2010.
15 Egan, *Bowie on Bowie*, p. 7.
16 Light, 'How David Bowie Brought the Thin White Duke to Life'.
17 Egan, *Bowie on Bowie*, p. 82.
18 Ibid., pp. 56–7.
19 Ibid., p. 324.
20 Ibid., pp. 39–40.

5 Bryan Ferry: 'When She Walks (in the Room)' (1978)

1 Bryan Ferry quoted in *New Musical Express*, 1 December 1972.
2 Michael Bracewell, *Roxy: The Band that Invented an Era* (London, 2007), p. 143.
3 Susan Sontag, 'Notes on Camp' [1964], in *Notes on Camp* (London, 2018), p. 4.
4 James Truman, *Details* (Condé Nast publication), May 1993.
5 Sontag, 'Notes on Camp', p. 5.
6 Ibid., p. 8.
7 Ibid., p. 29.
8 Ibid.
9 Tim Blanks, 'Bryan Ferry', *Anothermanmag* (Summer/Autumn 2020), www.anothermanmag.com.
10 Bryan Ferry interview, *Melody Maker*, 16 September 1978, np.
11 Ibid.
12 Ibid.

13 Ibid.

14 Ibid.

15 Ibid.

16 Barry Lazell and Dafydd Rees, *Bryan Ferry and Roxy Music* (London, 1982), p. 66.

17 James Truman, *Details*, May 1993.

6 Tom Waits: 'Ruby's Arms' (1980)

1 Barney Hoskyns, *Lowside of the Road: A Life of Tom Waits* (London, 2009), p. 239.

2 Stephen K. Peeples, 'Heartattack and Vine', in *Tom Waits on Tom Waits: Interviews and Encounters*, ed. Paul Maher Jr (London, 2011), p. 116.

3 Dave Zimmer, BAM, 26 February 1982.

4 Peeples, 'Heartattack and Vine', p. 114.

5 Jay S. Jacobs, *Wild Years: The Music and Myth of Tom Waits* (Toronto, 2006), p. 100.

6 Zimmer, BAM.

7 Ibid.

8 Ibid.

9 Ibid.

10 Peeples, 'Heartattack and Vine', p. 115.

11 Hoskyns, *Lowside of the Road*, p. 250.

12 Ibid.

13 Peeples, 'Heartattack and Vine', pp. 120–21.

14 Ibid.

15 Ibid.

16 Susan Sontag, 'Notes on Camp' [1964], in *Notes on Camp* (London, 2018), p. 20.

17 Ibid.

18 Zimmer, BAM.

19 Larry Blake interview, *Recording Engineer/Producer* (June 1982).

20 Peter Guttridge, 'A Simple Love Story', in *Tom Waits on Tom Waits*, ed. Paul Maher Jr, p. 125.

21 Richard M. Sudhalter, *Stardust Melody: The Life and Music of Hoagy Carmichael* (Oxford, 2002), p. 293.

22 Asked if he was familiar with Beefheart's music at this time, Waits replied, 'Nope. I became more acquainted with him when I got married. My wife [Kathleen Brennan] had all his records.' Mac Montandon, *Innocent When You Dream: The Tom Waits Reader* (London, 2007), p. 317. Driven by Beefheart, this next phase in

Waits's music would, in turn, feed through to Shane MacGowan's singing from 1985 onwards, when the Pogues constantly played Waits's follow-up to *Swordfishtrombones* – *Raindogs* (1985) – on their tour bus, an exchange Waits acknowledged with a cover version of their torch ballad 'Dirty Old Town' being performed on the *Big Time* tour in 1988. See James Fearnley, *Here Comes Everybody: The Story of the Pogues* (London, 2013), pp. 201–2.

23 Howard Larman, 'Interview with Tom Waits', in *Tom Waits on Tom Waits*, ed. Maher, p. 23.

24 Miles Davis, *Miles: The Autobiography* (New York, 1989), p. 385. In the same passage, Davis details the night Sinatra sent someone to Birdland to see if they could collaborate on an LP together.

25 Jack Kerouac, *Big Sur* [1962] (London, 2001), p. 55.

26 Bret Kofford, 'Tradition with a Twist', in *Tom Waits on Tom Waits*, ed. Maher, p. 294.

27 Mick Brown, 'My Wild Years and the Woman that Saved My Life', in *Tom Waits on Tom Waits*, ed. Maher, p. 441.

28 Hoskyns, *Lowside of the Road*, p. 117.

29 Jacobs, *Wild Years*, p. 43.

30 Hoskyns, *Lowside of the Road*, p. 40.

31 Ibid., p. 209.

32 Montandon, *Innocent When You Dream*, p. 119.

7 Grace Jones: 'Unlimited Capacity for Love' (1982)

1 Grace Jones, *I'll Never Write My Memoirs* (London, 2015), p. 231.

2 Nicole Pasulka, 'Militantly Naughty: Grace Jones and the Compass Point All-Stars', Red Bull Academy, www.redbullmusicacademy.com, 1 September 2016.

3 Ibid.

4 Mary Harron, 'Grace Jones: This Year's Model', *Smash Hits*, 4 September 1980, p. 22.

5 Mick McStarkey, 'What's that Sound?', *Far Out*, https://faroutmagazine.co.uk, 3 April 2021.

6 Benji B, 'Sly and Robbie', interview transcript available at www.redbullmusicacademy.com.

7 Pasulka, 'Militantly Naughty'.

8 Ibid.

9 Ibid.

10 Rob Tannenbaum, 'Wally Badarou's All-World Keyboards', *Musician* (May 1986), p. 40.

11 Jones, *I'll Never Write My Memoirs*, p. 213.

12 Ibid.
13 Ibid.
14 Ibid., p. 256.
15 Ibid., pp. 213–14.
16 Ibid., p. 283.
17 Ibid., pp. 204–5.
18 Chris Salewicz, 'Grace Jones: Confessions of an Art Groupie', *The Face* (October 1980), p. 52.
19 Jones, *I'll Never Write My Memoirs*, p. 222.
20 Iggy Pop, 'Frank Sinatra's *Only the Lonely* (1958)', https:// vinylwriters.com, accessed 12 October 2022.
21 Ronald Hart, 'Nightclubbing at 40: Grace Jones and the Compass Point All-Stars', www.passionweiss.com, accessed 11 October 2022.
22 Ibid.
23 McStarkey, 'What's that Sound?'
24 Hart, 'Nightclubbing at 40'.
25 Ibid.
26 Initially, producer Mark Miller Mundy attempted to put Faithfull together with elements of the Compass Point Allstars – primarily Dunbar and Shakespeare – in a gambit to bolster *Broken English* and make it too part of the current new wave/reggae interface. But Faithfull refused to have the LP's production shifted from London to Nassau, sensing the move would not benefit the gritty tone desired for *Broken English*.
27 Ronnie Gurr, 'The Devil in Ms Jones', *Record Mirror*, 23 August 1980, p. 12.
28 Ibid.
29 Benji B, 'Sly and Robbie'.
30 Ibid.
31 Jones, *I'll Never Write My Memoirs*, p. 221.
32 Hart, 'Nightclubbing at 40'.
33 Ibid.
34 Don Snowden, 'Grace Jones: New Wave for a Disco Diva', *Los Angeles Times*, 20 July 1980, p. 15.
35 Benji B, 'Sly and Robbie'.
36 Jones, *I'll Never Write My Memoirs*, p. 82.
37 Ibid., pp. 213–14.
38 Ibid., p. 223.
39 Ibid., p. 47.
40 Iman Lababedi, 'Grace Jones: Are You Ready for a Brand New (Disco) Beat?', *Creem* (April 1983).

41 Jones, *I'll Never Write My Memoirs*, p. 132.

42 Ibid.

43 Susan Sontag, 'Notes on Camp' [1964], in *Notes on Camp* (London, 2018), p. 8.

44 Ibid., p. 9.

45 Jones, *I'll Never Write My Memoirs*, p. 53.

8 Ian McCulloch: 'Ocean Rain' (1984)

1 Rod Kitson, 'Mouth of the Mersey: Ian McCulloch's Favourite Albums', *The Quietus*, https://thequietus.com, 21 March 2013.

2 Chris Adams, *Turquoise Days: The Weird World of Echo and the Bunnymen* (New York, 2002), p. 122.

3 Ibid.

4 *Ocean Rain* (Remastered) (Rhino Records, 2003), CD booklet.

5 Ibid.

6 Adams, *Turquoise Days*, p. 124.

7 See the references to Sinatra in Jerry Hopkins and Danny Sugerman's *No One Here Gets Out Alive* (London, 1980), pp. 107, 128, 188.

8 Adams, *Turquoise Days*, p. 5.

9 Ian McCulloch interviewed by Mary Anne Hobbs for Radio 6 Music, 16 March 2014, available online at www.bbc.co.uk.

10 The song appears on the Fun Lovin' Criminals LP *Mimosa* (Chrysalis, 1999).

11 James Kaplan, *Sinatra: The Chairman* (London, 2015), p. 698.

12 Adams, *Turquoise Days*, p. 53.

13 Ibid., p. 51.

14 Ibid., p. 151.

15 Ibid., p. 52.

16 Ibid., p. 151.

17 Ibid., p. 153.

18 Ibid., p. 154.

19 Ibid., p. 153.

20 Ibid., p. 156

21 Ibid., p. 130.

22 Ibid., p. 159.

23 'Ian McCulloch Interview with Jools Holland', www.youtube.com, 7 May 2012.

24 Adams, *Turquoise Days*, p. 159.

25 *Echo and the Bunnymen* (Remastered) (Rhino Records, 2003), CD booklet.

9 Nick Cave: 'Far from Me' (1997)

1 Mat Snow, *Nick Cave: Sinner Saint: The True Confessions* (London, 2011), p. 54.
2 Ibid., p. 140.
3 Ibid., p. 163.
4 'Nick Cave on Working with Johnny Cash', *Uncut*, www.uncut.co.uk, 22 January 2009.
5 Johnny Cash, *Cash: The Autobiography* (London, 2000), p. 58.
6 Snow, *Nick Cave*, p. 172.
7 Ibid., p. 138.
8 Sylvie Simmons, *I'm Your Man: The Life of Leonard Cohen* (London, 2012), p. 361.
9 Ian Johnston, *Bad Seed: The Biography of Nick Cave* (London, 1995), p. 153.
10 Simmons, *I'm Your Man*, p. 202.
11 Nick Cave, 'What Does Elvis Mean to You?', *The Red Hand Files*, 34 (April 2019), www.theredhandfiles.com.
12 Ibid.
13 Johnston, *Bad Seed*, p. 260.
14 Snow, *Nick Cave*, p. 76.
15 Ibid., pp. 70, 174.
16 'Nick Cave Interview with Nanni Jacobson, Los Angeles, 1997', www.youtube.com, accessed 10 October 2022.
17 Snow, *Nick Cave: Sinner Saint*, pp. 170–71.
18 Ibid., p. 86.
19 Nick Cave, 'Your Relationship with PJ Harvey', *The Red Hand Files*, 57 (August 2019), www.theredhandfiles.com.
20 Snow, *Nick Cave*, p. 173.
21 Ibid., p. 61.
22 Ibid., p. 62.

10 Nas: 'Bye Baby' (2012)

1 The most reliable first-hand reminiscences of Sinatra appear in Pete Hamill, *Why Sinatra Matters* (New York, 1998).
2 Nas composed a song about Rakim: 'U.B.R. (Unauthorized Biography of Rakim)', featured on *Street's Disciple* (Columbia, 2004).
3 Rakim, *Sweat the Technique: Revelations on Creativity* (New York, 2019), p. 18.
4 Ibid., p. 68.

5 Michael Eric Dyson and Sohail Daulatzai, *Born to Use Mics: Reading Nas's 'Illmatic'* (New York, 2010), p. 274.
6 'Nas on Marvin Gaye's Marriage, Parenting and Rap Genius', NPR, www.npr.org, 20 July 2012.
7 Keith Murphy, 'Nas Opens Up about Personal Moments on *Life Is Good* Album', *Billboard*, www.billboard.com, 29 June 2012.
8 Gerrick D. Kennedy, 'A Conversation with Nas', *Los Angeles Times*, 20 August 2012.
9 'Nas on Marvin Gaye's Marriage, Parenting and Rap Genius'.
10 Jan Gaye, *After the Dance: My Life with Marvin Gaye* (New York, 2013), p. 182.
11 David Ritz, *Divided Soul: The Life of Marvin Gaye* (Boston, MA, 1991), p. 29.
12 More ambivalent is Sinatra's mid-tempo version of Cole Porter's 'Just One of Those Things' (1954), accentuated when the song is treated as a ballad during a live show in Vegas in 1961. This version finds Sinatra negotiating the fine line between the torch ballad and the kiss-off song with an increased level of subtlety.
13 'Nas on Marvin Gaye's Marriage, Parenting and Rap Genius'.
14 Pete Hamill, *Why Sinatra Matters* (New York, 1998), p. 19.
15 Dyson and Daulatzai, *Born to Use Mics*, p. 230.
16 Ibid.
17 'Nas on Marvin Gaye's Marriage, Parenting and Rap Genius'.
18 Ibid.
19 Ibid.
20 Ben Edmonds, *Marvin Gaye: What's Going On and the Last Days of the Motown Sound* (Edinburgh, 2001), pp. 173–4.
21 Miles Davis, *Miles: The Autobiography* (New York, 1989), p. 60.
22 Dyson and Daulatzai, *Born to Use Mics*, p. 229.

Conclusion

1 Anthony Reynolds, *The Impossible Dream: The Story of Scott Walker and the Walker Brothers* (London, 2009), p. 135.
2 David Ritz, *Divided Soul: The Life of Marvin Gaye* (Boston, MA, 1991), p. 29.
3 Ibid., pp. 39–40.
4 Bryan Ferry quoted in *New Musical Express*, 1 December 1972.
5 Bret Kofford, 'Tradition with a Twist', in *Tom Waits on Tom Waits: Interviews and Encounters*, ed. Paul Maher Jr (London, 2011), p. 294.
6 Grace Jones, *I'll Never Write My Memoirs* (London, 2015), p. 222.

7 Rod Kitson, 'Mouth of the Mersey: Ian McCulloch's Favourite Albums', *The Quietus*, https://thequietus.com, 21 March 2013.

8 Mat Snow, *Nick Cave: Sinner Saint: The True Confessions* (London, 2011), p. 61.

9 Ibid., p. 68.

10 The two key contemporary Sinatra historians are Will Friedwald, *The Song Is You: A Singer's Art* (New York, 1995), and James Kaplan, *Sinatra: The Chairman* (London, 2015). One of the few essays to fairly take on Sinatra's output from the late 1960s is Gene Lees, 'Frank Sinatra: Confessions and Contradictions' [1969], in *The Frank Sinatra Reader*, ed. Steven Petkov and Leonard Mustazza (New York, 1995), pp. 139–42.

11 Simon Frith, *Performing Rites: Evaluating Popular Music* (Oxford, 1996), pp. 188–9, 190, 199; Simon Reynolds, *Rip It Up and Start Again: Post-Punk, 1978–1984* (London, 2005), pp. 440, 454.

Select Bibliography

Adams, Chris, *Turquoise Days: The Weird World of Echo and the Bunnymen*
(New York, 2002)
Bracewell, Michael, *Roxy: The Band that Invented an Era* (London, 2007)
Dyson, Michael Eric, and Sohail Daulatzai, *Born to Use Mics: Reading Nas's
Illmatic* (New York, 2010)
Egan, Sean, *Bowie on Bowie: Interviews and Encounters with David Bowie*
(London, 2015)
Friedwald, Will, *Sinatra! The Song Is You* (New York, 1997)
Hamill, Pete, *Why Sinatra Matters* (New York, 1998)
Hoskyns, Barney, *Lowside of the Road: A Life of Tom Waits* (London, 2009)
Johnston, Ian, *Bad Seed: The Biography of Nick Cave* (London, 1995)
Jones, Dylan, *David Bowie: A Life* (London, 2017)
Jones, Grace, *I'll Never Write My Memoirs* (London, 2015)
Kaplan, James, *Sinatra: The Chairman* (New York, 2015)
Lazell, Barry, and Dafydd Rees, *Bryan Ferry and Roxy Music* (London,
1982)
Maher, Paul Jr, *Tom Waits on Tom Waits: Interviews and Encounters*
(London, 2011)
Reed, Jeremy, *Another Tear Falls: A Study of Scott Walker* (London, 1998)
Reynolds, Anthony, *The Impossible Dream: The Story of Scott Walker and
the Walker Brothers* (London, 2009)
Rubython, Tom, *White Music: The Barry White Story* (Northamptonshire,
2017)
Snow, Mat, *Nick Cave: Sinner Saint: The True Confessions* (London, 2011)
White, Barry, *Love Unlimited: Insights on Life and Love* (New York, 1999)

Select Discography

Bowie, David, *Young Americans* (1975)
—, *Station to Station* (1976)
Echo and the Bunnymen, *Heaven Up Here* (1981)
—, *Ocean Rain* (1984)
Ferry, Bryan, *Another Time/Another Place* (1974)
—, *The Bridge Stripped Bare* (1978)
Jones, Grace, *Nightclubbing* (1981)
—, *Living My Life* (1982)
Nas, *Illmatic* (1994)
—, *Life Is Good* (2012)
Nick Cave and the Bad Seeds, *Kicking Against the Pricks* (1986)
—, *The Boatman's Call* (1997)
Sinatra, Frank, *In the Wee Small Hours* (1955)
—, *Where Are You?* (1957)
—, *Only the Lonely* (1958)
—, *A Man Alone* (1969)
Waits, Tom, *One from the Heart* (1982)
—, *Heartattack and Vine* (1980)
Walker, Scott, *Scott 3* (1969)
—, *Scott 4* (1969)
White, Barry, *I've Got So Much to Give* (1973)
—, *Let the Music Play* (1976)

Acknowledgements

For reading specific chapters, thanks go to David Blamey, Michael Bracewell, Adam Bradley, James Dyer, Gary Finnegan, Rupert Howe, Charlie Jackson, Helen Kincaid, Simon Morrison, Rick Poynor and Tom Wilcox.

For reading the entire manuscript, thanks to Paul Dale, Sophie McKinlay and especially John Scanlan.

At Reaktion Books, my thanks go to Michael Leaman, Amy Salter and proofreader Camilla Gersh.

Photo Acknowledgements

The authors and publishers wish to thank the relevant organizations and individuals listed below for authorizing reproduction of their work.

Alamy: pp. 13 (AJ Pics), 27 (All Star Picture Library), 28 (Science History Images), 44 (Pictorial Press Ltd), 63 (Keystone Press), 75 (Gijsbert Hanekroot), 84 (Records), 90 (Pictorial Press Ltd), 94 (Cinematic Collection), 102 (Pictorial Press Ltd), 105 (Keystone Press), 106 (PBH Images), 116 (Picture-Lux/The Hollywood Archive), 120 (CBW), 144 (Moviestore Collection), 153 (East News sp. z o. o.), 158 (Gonzales Photo), 161 (The Photo Access); Getty Images: pp. 6 (Bettmann), 15 (Bettmann), 43 (Hulton Archive), 55 (David Redfern), 68 (Bobby Holland/Michael Ochs Archives), 72 (Michael Ochs Archive), 76 (Mark Sullivan), 80 (CBS Photo Archive), 87 (Ian Dickson/ Redferns), 113 (George Rose), 128 (Steve Rapport), 131 (Steve Rapport), 139 (Steve Rapport), 147 (K&K Ulf Kruger OHG), 154 (Dave Tonge); Library of Congress, Washington, DC: p. 24; Wikimedia Commons: pp. 10 (Public Domain), 40 (Public Domain), 57 (John H. White/Public Domain), 110 (Gary Friedman, Los Angeles Times/CC BY-SA 4.0 International), 156 (MikaV/CC BY-SA 4.0 International), 167 (Mikamote/CC BY-SA 3.0 Unported).

Index

Page numbers in *italics* indicate illustrations